GUIDE TO GENEALOGY

T. J. Resler

NATIONAL GEOGRAPHIC KIDS

WASHINGTON, D.C.

CONTENTS

INTRODUCTION

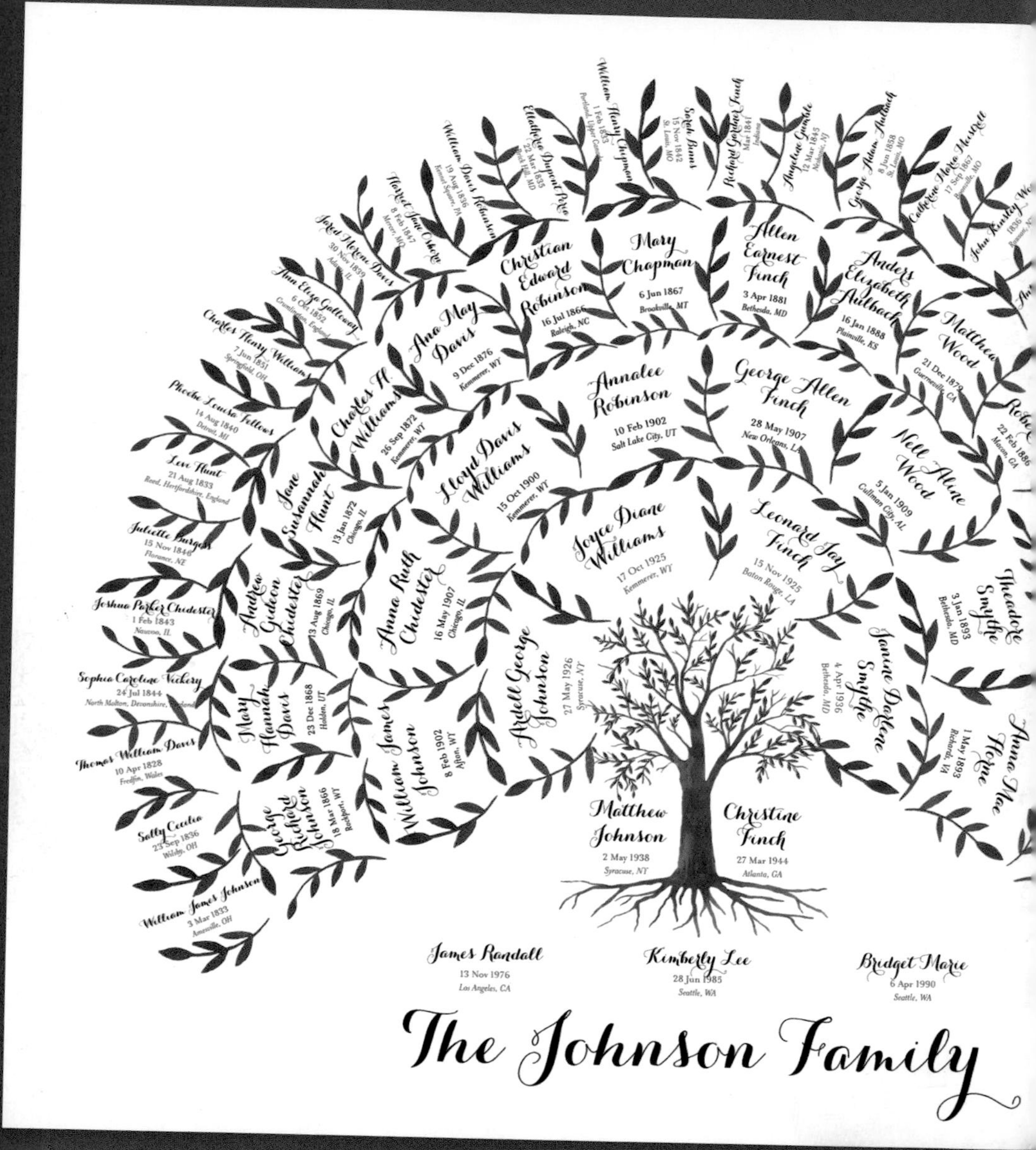

A family tree is a diagram that shows how people in multiple generations of a family are related to one another. It's also a fun way to see your family heritage! Family trees can actually look like trees, as in this example, or they can be organized in other shapes, such as a fan, a bow tie, or an hourglass. See more about filling in your family tree on pages 44–45.

WHO ARE YOU?

IF YOU'VE EVER PUZZLED OVER YOUR ORIGINS OR HOW YOUR FAMILY ENDED UP WHERE IT DID, YOU'RE A NATURAL GENEALOGIST.

Genealogists study and trace their families back generations to learn more about their unique stories and to put together all the branches of their family tree. Genealogy is like detective work. You follow clues, dig up evidence, and build a case. Along the way, you uncover secrets, separate fact from fiction, and discover amazing stories about your ancestors. It takes smarts, dedication, and skill. In other words, it takes you.

This book will help you investigate your family's past. It'll turn you into a genealogical detective. It'll show you the techniques to investigate your heritage: how to discover evidence, evaluate it, and keep track of it. You'll learn how to interview witnesses and where to find clues—and what's online and what's not. You'll get clued in about where to start your investigation and how to link generations so you don't investigate the wrong people. This book will be your sidekick as you dig deep into the key evidence that frames your ancestors' lives and uncover the resources that reveal their life stories. It'll also take you into the lab, where you'll learn about genetic genealogy, using your DNA to find your ancestors—even those from long, long ago. Along the way, you'll learn about the waves of immigration that may have brought your ancestors to America, whether they were early arrivals or relative newcomers, and you'll discover ways to get around the roadblocks that trip up other genealogical detectives. As you learn about your ancestors, you'll also learn about *you*. So the next time someone asks, "Who are you?" you'll have an amazing answer.

HOW TO USE THIS BOOK

THIS BOOK IS PACKED with features to help you become a great genealogical detective. Check them out!

GET CLUED IN bullets give you the facts and techniques you'll need for your genealogical investigation.

HIT THE BOOKS

THERE ARE MAGICAL PLACES FILLED WITH EVIDENCE ABOUT YOUR HERITAGE. Maybe you've heard of them. They're called ... drumroll ... libraries. Many libraries and archives have dedicated collections of genealogical materials or terrific collections of family histories and local histories that may shed light on your ancestors' lives. Besides books, libraries have rare manuscripts, special genealogical journals and magazines, and one-of-a-kind materials—evidence you won't find on the Internet. In addition to public libraries and archives, check out the collections of some private libraries and lineage societies. Some libraries are so good that genealogists travel across the country to visit them!

96

GET CLUED IN

- **Big, small, and specialized.** Large libraries often have impressive genealogical collections covering a broad region and many years. But don't overlook small, local libraries and historical societies! They may have great information about families who lived in their area. Many libraries have a guidebook or pamphlet (hard copy and online) that tells you what kind of materials they have and how to find them. Also, be sure to look through the library's catalog, the database of everything it has in its collection, which often is digitized and available online, even if the materials themselves are not.
- **Your new BFF.** Some of the best resources in libraries and archives aren't dusty old books and microfilm. They're people! Professional librarians and archivists have advanced training in how to do research. They're happy to help you find resources for your genealogical detective work. Some libraries even let you email a question to a librarian. They won't do the research for you, but they'll point you to where you can find the information you need. That kind of help will make you best friends forever!
- **It's too far away!** If you can't travel to a distant library, you may be able to borrow some books through an interlibrary loan service. The distant library will send the book to your local library, if both participate in the service. A word of warning: Reference books, including some genealogy books, often cannot be checked out or obtained through interlibrary loan. But many materials can. The Family History Library sends materials to its branches all over the world. The St. Louis County Library, which obtained the National Genealogical Society's Collection, lends out those 28,000 books, too.

GET SMART FAST

INVESTIGATE	CLUES
Family History Library, Salt Lake City, Utah, the world's largest genealogical library familysearch.org	Huge collection of primary sources, including U.S. federal, state, and county records, family histories, and maps
Library of Congress, Washington, D.C., the world's largest library loc.gov	One of the world's premier collections of U.S. and [illegible] genealogical collections, with directories, newspapers, photos, and maps
National Archives, Washington, D.C. U.S. government records archives.gov	Census records, military service records, immigration and naturalization records
New York Public Library, New York, New York nypl.org	One of the largest genealogical collections, especially related to New York, Irish, and African-American sources
New England Historic Genealogical Society Research Library, Boston, Massachusetts americanancestors.org	New England records; materials back to the 14th century; extensive Canadian, Irish, and British collections
Mid-Continent Public Library Midwest Genealogy Center, Independence, Missouri mymcpl.org/genealogy	Materials on American slave trade, antebellum South, Southeast, mid-Atlantic, Midwest, and Plains states

EXPERT TIP

YOU CAN SEARCH THE COLLECTIONS OF THOUSANDS OF LIBRARIES AT ONCE AT [illegible] WORLD'S LARGEST NETWORK OF [illegible] CONTENT. THE [illegible] WILL EVEN TELL YOU THE CLOSEST [illegible] THAT HAS THE INFORMATION YOU WANT.

GET SMART FAST boxes provide fast facts about what to investigate and related clues. For all the websites in this book, be sure you go online with a parent or other trusted adult.

FUN FACTS and **DID YOU KNOW?** features give you fun and unique bits of information related to the topic.

EXPERT TIPS teach you the little tricks that help you get the most out of your investigation.

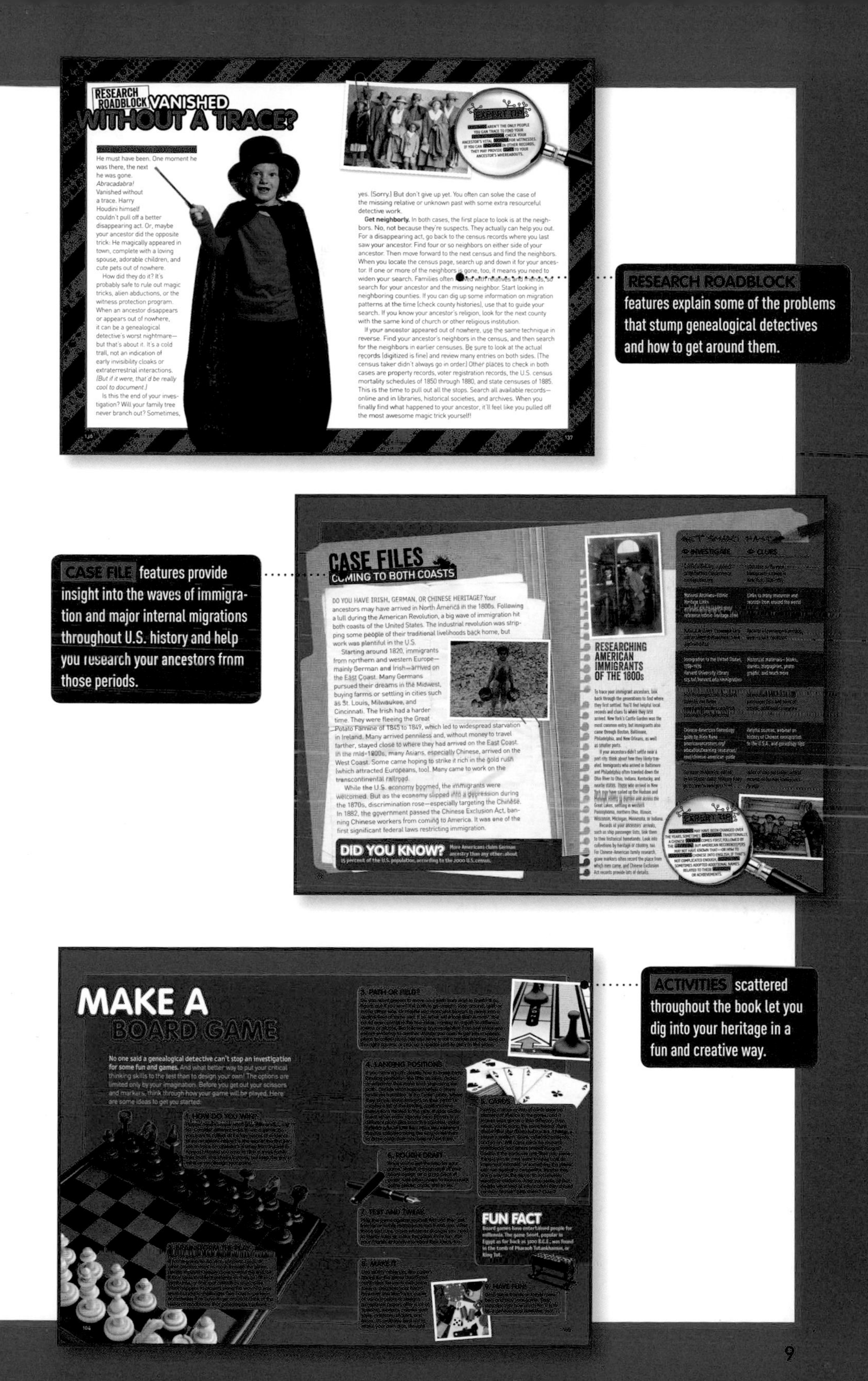

RESEARCH ROADBLOCK

VANISHED WITHOUT A TRACE?

He must have been. One moment he was there, the next he was gone. *Abracadabra!* Vanished without a trace. Harry Houdini himself couldn't pull off a better disappearing act. Or, maybe your ancestor did the opposite trick: He magically appeared in town, complete with a loving spouse, adorable children, and cute pets out of nowhere.

How did they do it? It's probably safe to rule out magic tricks, alien abductions, or the witness protection program. When an ancestor disappears or appears out of nowhere, it can be a genealogical detective's worst nightmare—but that's about it. It's a cold trail, not an indication of early invisibility cloaks or extraterrestrial interactions. *(But if it were, that'd be really cool to document.)*

Is this the end of your investigation? Will your family tree never branch out? Sometimes, yes. (Sorry.) But don't give up yet. You often can solve the case of the missing relative or unknown past with some extra resourceful detective work.

Get neighborly. In both cases, the first place to look is at the neighbors. No, not because they're suspects. They actually can help you out. For a disappearing act, go back to the census records where you last saw your ancestor. Find four or so neighbors on either side of your ancestor. Then move forward to the next census and find the neighbors. When you locate the census page, search up and down it for your ancestor. If one or more of the neighbors is gone, too, it means you need to widen your search. Families often moved with relatives and friends, so search for your ancestor and the missing neighbor. Start looking in neighboring counties. If you can dig up some information on migration patterns at the time (check county histories), use that to guide your search. If you know your ancestor's religion, look for the next county with the same kind of church or other religious institution.

If your ancestor appeared out of nowhere, use the same technique in reverse. Find your ancestor's neighbors in the census, and then search for the neighbors in earlier censuses. Be sure to look at the actual records (digitized is fine) and review many entries on both sides. (The census taker didn't always go in order.) Other places to check in both cases are property records, voter registration records, the U.S. census mortality schedules of 1850 through 1880, and state censuses of 1885. This is the time to pull out all the stops. Search all available records—online and in libraries, historical societies, and archives. When you finally find what happened to your ancestor, it'll feel like you pulled off the most awesome magic trick yourself!

136 137

RESEARCH ROADBLOCK features explain some of the problems that stump genealogical detectives and how to get around them.

CASE FILE features provide insight into the waves of immigration and major internal migrations throughout U.S. history and help you research your ancestors from those periods.

CASE FILES
COMING TO BOTH COASTS

DO YOU HAVE IRISH, GERMAN, OR CHINESE HERITAGE? Your ancestors may have arrived in North America in the 1800s. Following a lull during the American Revolution, a big wave of immigration hit both coasts of the United States. The industrial revolution was stripping some people of their traditional livelihoods back home, but work was plentiful in the U.S.

Starting around 1820, immigrants from northern and western Europe—mainly German and Irish—arrived on the East Coast. Many Germans pursued their dreams in the Midwest, buying farms or settling in cities such as St. Louis, Milwaukee, and Cincinnati. The Irish had a harder time. They were fleeing the Great Potato Famine of 1845 to 1849, which led to widespread starvation in Ireland. Many arrived penniless and, without money to travel farther, stayed close to where they had arrived on the East Coast. In the mid-1800s, many Asians, especially Chinese, arrived on the West Coast. Some came hoping to strike it rich in the gold rush (which attracted Europeans, too). Many came to work on the transcontinental railroad.

While the U.S. economy boomed, the immigrants were welcomed. But as the economy slipped into a depression during the 1870s, discrimination rose—especially targeting the Chinese. In 1882, the government passed the Chinese Exclusion Act, banning Chinese workers from coming to America. It was one of the first significant federal laws restricting immigration.

DID YOU KNOW? More Americans claim German ancestry than any other: about 15 percent of the U.S. population, according to the 2000 U.S. census.

RESEARCHING AMERICAN IMMIGRANTS OF THE 1800s

MAKE A BOARD GAME

No one said a genealogical detective can't stop an investigation for some fun and games. And what better way to put your critical thinking skills to the test than to design your own! The options are limited only by your imagination. Before you get out your scissors and markers, think through how your game will be played. Here are some ideas to get you started:

FUN FACT Board games have entertained people for millennia. The game Senet, popular in Egypt as far back as 3500 B.C.E., was found in the tomb of Pharaoh Tutankhamun, or King Tut.

ACTIVITIES scattered throughout the book let you dig into your heritage in a fun and creative way.

ON THE MOVE

"WHO ARE YOU?" IT SOUNDS LIKE A SIMPLE QUESTION. But to answer it, you need to tackle another question first: "Where do you come from?" You might be tempted to rattle off a list of places you or your parents have lived, but that's not the whole picture, is it? Chances are, your parents' families originated somewhere else, such as Europe, Africa, Asia, or Latin America. And no matter how long their families lived in the "old country," they weren't always from there either.

Since the earliest days of human existence, we've been on the move. If you go back far enough—really far, like 200,000 to 60,000 years ago—our ancestors were in Africa. Yep, all of them. Scientists who study our genetic heredity can trace our families' journeys over thousands of years, thanks to little markers encoded in our genetic makeup. And all those journeys started in eastern Africa. Africa was drying out, and our very distant ancestors began to leave eastern Africa about 60,000 years ago. Some of them journeyed into other areas of Africa; others left the continent. They traveled up into the Middle East and then east along the coast of South Asia and, thousands of years later, even reached Australia. Another group left around 50,000 years ago and went to the Middle East and then to Central Asia. Within 15,000 years of leaving Africa, some of our distant ancestors made it to Europe, then farther into Asia. Much later—but still more than 15,000 years ago—some of those people walked from Asia across a temporary land bridge to America.

DID YOU KNOW?

When you move from one place to another and intend to stay there—not just take a vacation—you're migrating. Depending on where you are in your journey, you can call yourself either an immigrant or an emigrant. But which one and when? How do you keep it all straight? Here's a trick: Focus on the first letter. **M**igration refers to the **m**ovement. An **i**mmigrant is someone who comes *into* a country, while an **e**migrant is someone who leaves—or ***exits***—a country.

PUSH AND PULL. These very distant ancestors of ours left eastern Africa because changes in the climate made their lives difficult. They went in search of food and water—and better lives. It's a story that has played out over and over again in the history of human existence. Large migrations occur when hardship—drought, famine, or conflict—*pushes* people to leave their homes, or when opportunities elsewhere *pull* them toward a new home.

Fast forward several thousand years, and maybe your closer ancestors—the ones you can track through your genealogical detective work—may have been pushed from Ireland because of the Potato Famine or from Southeast Asia by conflict or natural disasters. Or maybe your ancestors were pulled by the cheap, plentiful land in a young America or job opportunities during various decades in the United States.

IMMIGRANT NATIONS. Though every country gets its share of immigrants, the United States, Canada, and Australia are often called "immigrant nations." In the past, each of these countries encouraged immigrants to come and settle there, and each experienced several waves of immigration over the past few centuries. Immigration played such an important part in those countries' founding and development that it shaped their answer to the question, "Who are we?" People living in some other countries say they're a nation because they "share common blood," but the United States, Canada, and Australia have looked at it differently. They had to unite diverse citizens by their allegiance to a common home. "We the People" included immigrants, including our ancestors.

EARLY MIGRANTS

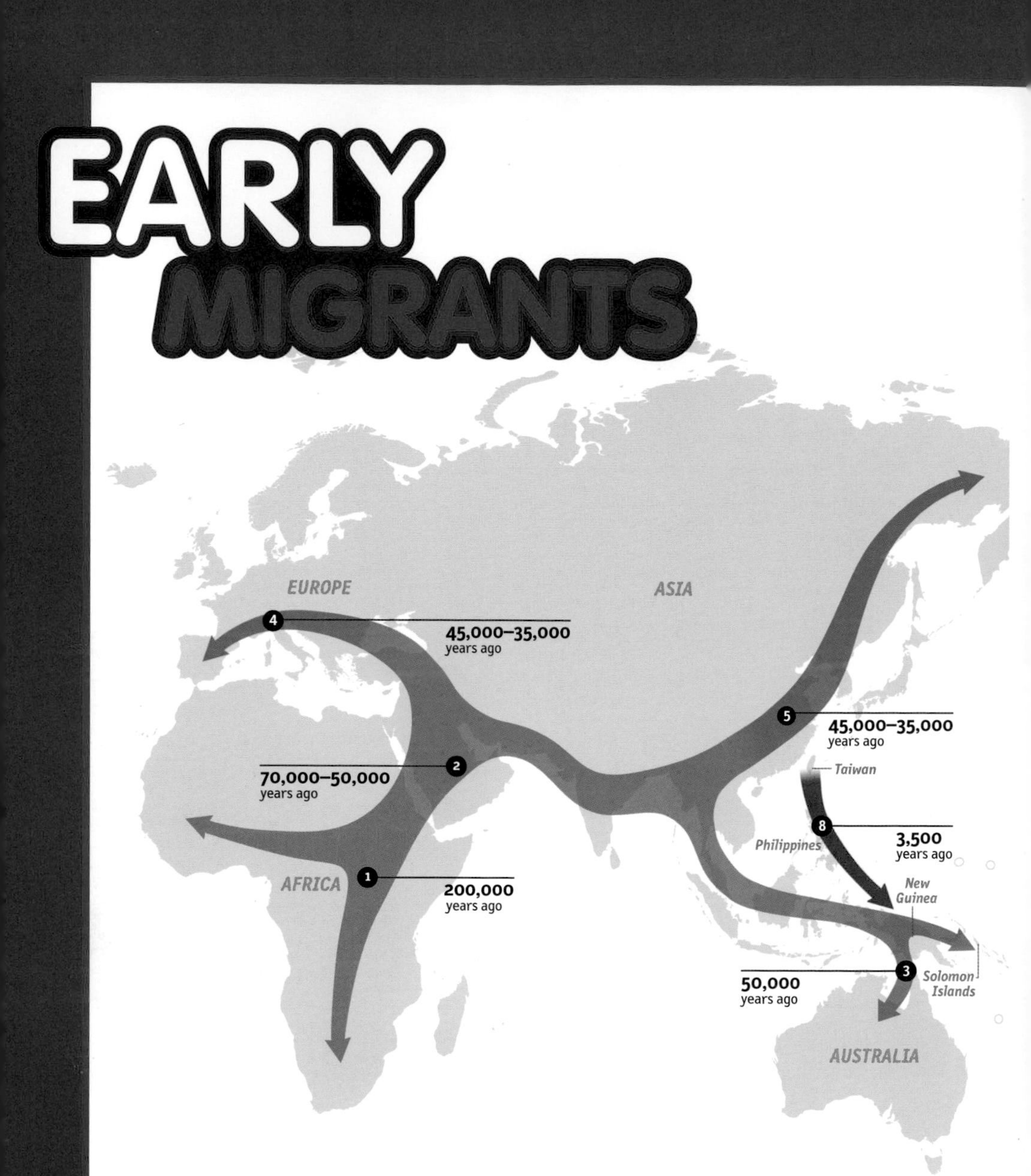

WE ALL TRACE OUR EARLIEST ANCESTORS TO EASTERN AFRICA. Around 60,000 years ago, our ancestors began to migrate in successive waves into new territories. Eventually they spread throughout the entire world. Except Antarctica—that's still just penguin territory.

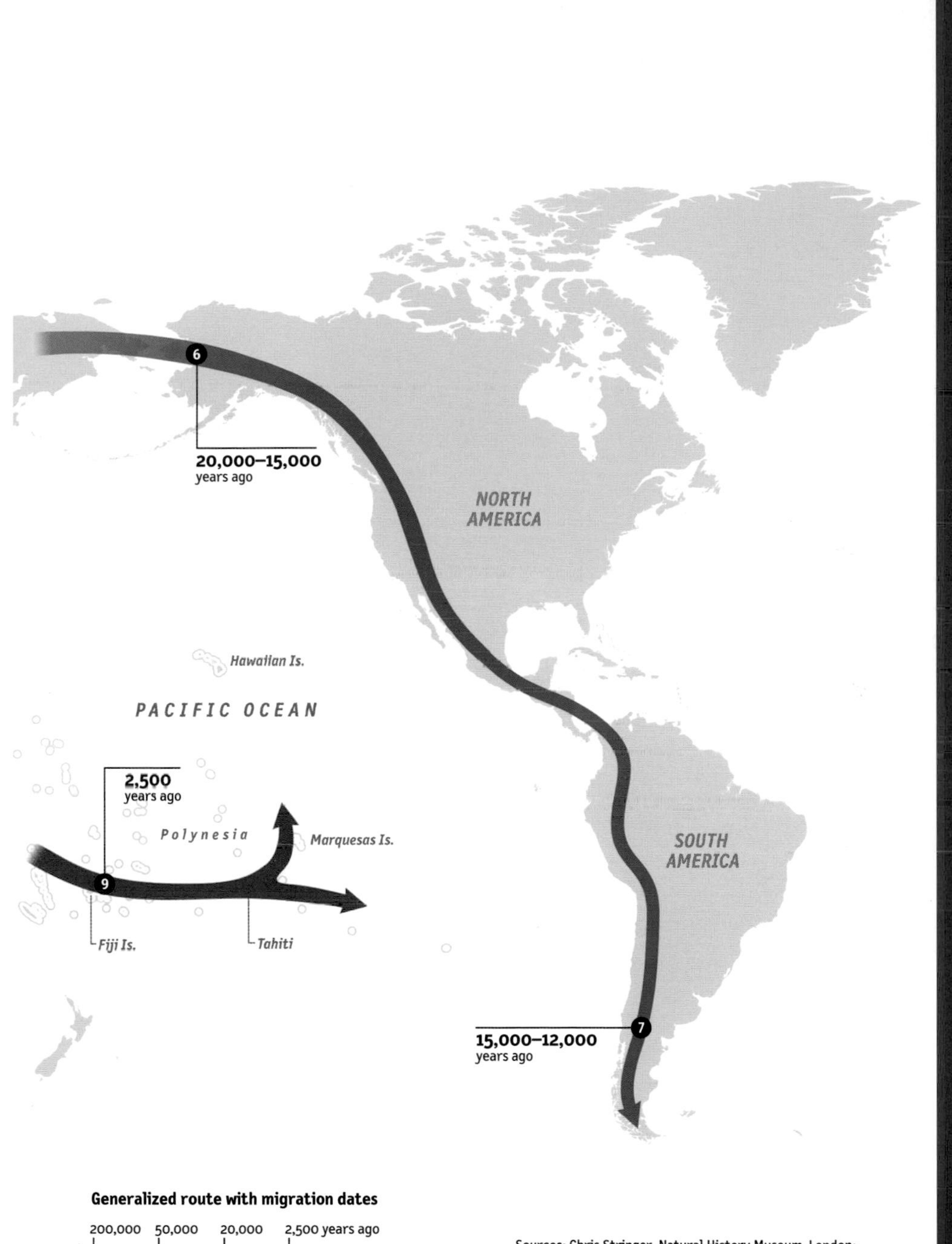

Sources: Chris Stringer, Natural History Museum, London; Spencer Wells, NG Staff

DETECTIVE WORK

Following clues, tracking down long-lost ancestors, uncovering secrets—that's what genealogy is all about. In this chapter, you'll get started on your genealogical detective case. You'll learn how to home in on a family mystery, develop detective techniques, and evaluate evidence so you can make a case for who you really are.

SOLVING A MYSTERY

YOUR FAMILY HISTORY IS MOSTLY A MYSTERY. Maybe you already know some of its stand-out stories—an ancestor who struck it rich in California's gold rush, a relative who fought in the French Revolution—and you can't wait to discover the juicy details. Or maybe you're a bit skeptical. You're thinking, My family? BOR-ING. Guess what? It's not! Families are full of secrets, harrowing journeys, and intriguing tales. You just haven't uncovered the good stuff ... yet. Whether you already know a lot or hardly anything at all, it's time to get cracking. The case awaits.

EXPERT TIP

LIKE ALL GOOD DETECTIVES, SET ASIDE WHAT YOU THINK YOU ALREADY KNOW. YOU'RE GOING TO FOLLOW COLD, HARD FACTS TO SOLVE YOUR MYSTERY. APPROACH THIS CASE WITH FRESH EYES, NOT PRECONCEIVED NOTIONS ABOUT WHAT YOU'LL FIND. THAT'S THE KEY TO SUCCESS.

A NOBLE EFFORT

For centuries in Europe, genealogy could determine whether you had wealth, status, and power—or even a right to sit on a throne. Royal or noble lineage (or "royal blood") entitled you to many privileges in society, though sometimes only if you were male and the firstborn in your family. The family line determined which member of a royal family would be the next monarch. For nobles—your barons, duchesses, counts, earls, and the like—documenting family lines showed who had legitimate claim to inherit property, wealth, and a privileged status in society. By the 21st century, nobility didn't guarantee power and wealth in most places. But many people would still love to claim a noble lineage.

GET CLUED IN

- **Focus.** One of your first decisions is how to focus your investigation. When you dig into your family's past, it's easy to get swamped with information. Your family tree branches out fast! Getting all the details on your grandparents may be manageable, but go back a couple more generations—to your great-great-grandparents—and you're already up to 16 people. Even if your ultimate goal is the tallest, bushiest family tree possible, start simply. (See page 114 for how to build your family tree.)

FUN FACT

The family tree of the great Chinese philosopher Confucius, born in 551 B.C.E., includes 83 generations and more than two million descendants. The tree, believed to be the world's largest, is 43,000 pages long!

- **Persons of interest.** A great way to start is to follow one line of your family. Which one is up to you. Maybe you stick to ancestors with your last name, or perhaps you focus on someone you know has a fascinating story. Are you named after a relative? You may want to trace your connection to your namesake. Be creative. If your mom has commented that you draw or sprint "just like Great-Aunt Katharine," why not work your way along her branch of the family tree? Maybe you'll find you come from a long line of artists or athletes.

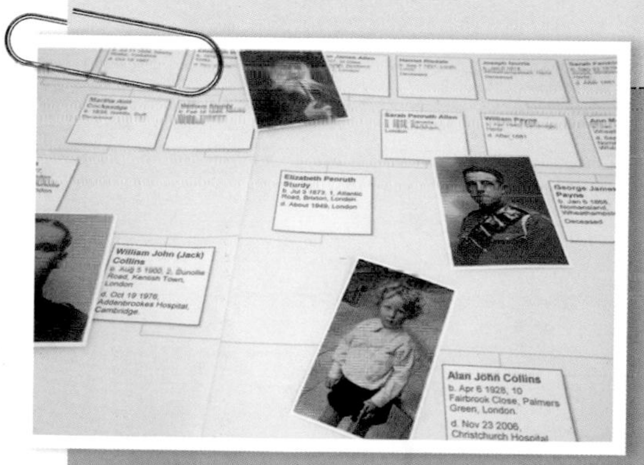

- **Branching out.** At some point, you'll want to branch out and include more relatives. Not only will it help your tree leaf out, it will also help your investigation. Learning details about your grandparents' siblings will tell you more about your grandparents' lives, too—and your heritage. Plus, important clues, such as family records or photographs, may have passed to these people's descendants instead of your parents. These are all pieces in your puzzle.

- **Family Ties.** Who goes in your family tree? Back when your grandparents were born, most kids grew up in a home with two parents who were married to each other and biologically related to their children. But today there is no such "typical" family structure. Many families have one parent, others have stepparents. Some kids are related to their parents genetically, others are not. Include all these connections. Family is not just about bloodlines.

KINDS OF KIN

ANCESTORS, COUSINS, RELATIVES, STEPPARENTS, ADOPTED SISTERS, HALF BROTHERS—THEY'RE ALL PART OF YOUR FAMILY. But how are they connected? Let's sort it out. But first, let's make sure we're clear on our terms. You may have heard a lot of these words before, but genealogical detectives need to be precise, so let's define some terms that'll pop up throughout this book.

GET CLUED IN

- **Adopted.** In families, it means someone who was brought into the family, but not born into it.
- **Ancestor.** Someone you're descended from—usually someone further back than your grandparents. You're that person's descendant.
- **Biological.** When talking about families, it means someone who's genetically related to you, not someone related through adoption or solely through marriage.

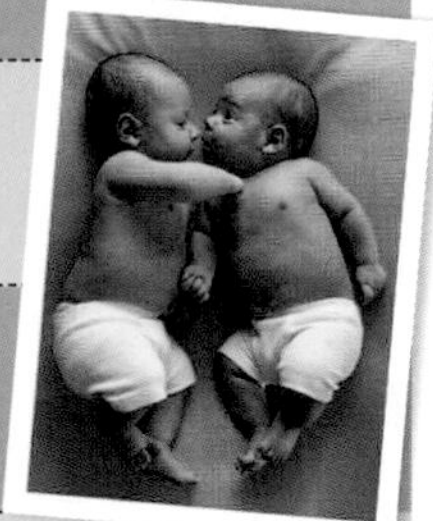

- **Close connections.** Your siblings (brothers and sisters), aunts and uncles, parents and grandparents are all close relatives.
- **Collateral relative.** Someone who shares one of your ancestors but is not in your direct family line.
- **Cousin.** Someone with whom you share at least one common ancestor.

- **Half-.** A half brother or half sister shares with you one—not both—of your biological parents.
- **Relative.** Any family member.
- **Step-.** Someone, like a stepdad or stepbrother, who became part of your family through marriage but is not biologically related to you.

ONE BIG FAMILY

How many ancestors do you have? It may seem simple to calculate. After all, each of us has two biological parents. They each had two parents, giving us four grandparents. They in turn had two parents (our eight great-grandparents) and so on and so forth. Keep crunching on that calculator back 30 generations (to around the year 1200 C.E.) and you get 1,073,741,824 ancestors! But, wait, there's a problem. That's more than the total population of the world at that time. What's going on? Your family tree doesn't keep branching out forever. It does for a while, but then it slows and starts to narrow back in, creating more of a diamond shape than an ever expanding triangle. Instead of having a bunch of separate branches, your family tree becomes more like an overlapping web. The same ancestors pop up on multiple family lines, causing a situation genealogists call "pedigree collapse." It happens when cousins marry each other—a practice more common than you may think. One researcher believes it's likely that 80 percent of all marriages in history were between second cousins or closer, and some geneticists believe everyone on Earth is at least a 50th cousin to everyone else. That means you can definitely say you're connected to royalty! (Probably pirates, too.)

QUICK QUIZ:

Meet Your Cousins

Who's your third cousin twice removed? If your eyes just glazed over, you're not alone. It can be hard to keep track of cousins. But here are some quick clues that will help.

Ordinals. The ordinal numbers—the "second," "third," and so on—tell you how closely related your cousin is to you. Your first cousin is your closest. But what exactly does "close" mean? It's how many generations you have to go back to find the ancestor you and your cousin have in common. Here's a quick way to figure it out: The ordinal number matches the number of "g" words in your common ancestor's title (in English). So, you and your fourth cousin have a common great-great-great-grandparent, while you and your first cousin share a grandparent.

Removals. Being "removed" doesn't mean your cousin was plucked off your family tree! It's a term that means you and your cousin are from different generations, relative to your common ancestor. "Once removed" means there's only one generation difference, like your great-great-grandparent is your cousin's great-great-great-grandparent. "Twice removed" means a two-generation difference, so add another "great" for your cousin.

Mystery solved: Your third cousin twice removed is ... drum roll ... the great-great-great-great-grandchild of your great-great-grandparent (the ancestor you have in common). Whew!

DID YOU KNOW?

Cell phones aren't the only things with 3G and 4G connections. Instead of writing "great-great-great-great-grandmother," genealogists write "4G-grandmother." It's a speedy way to talk about generations—not, in this case, about data speeds. Your 4G-grandma didn't have a cell phone!

DETECTIVE TECHNIQUES

EXPERT TIP

GENEALOGISTS HAVE TO WRITE DOWN DETAILS FOR ALL SORTS OF EVIDENCE: DOCUMENTS, TOMBSTONES, PHOTOGRAPHS, INTERVIEWS, AND MORE. ONE GO-TO SOURCE FOR FORMATTING ALL THOSE SOURCE CITATIONS IS *EVIDENCE EXPLAINED: CITING HISTORY SOURCES FROM ARTIFACTS TO CYBERSPACE* BY ELIZABETH SHOWN MILLS. SHE ALSO HAS A WEBSITE, EVIDENCEEXPLAINED.COM, WITH HELPFUL TIPS.

DETECTIVE WORK IS ALL ABOUT GATHERING AND EVALUATING EVIDENCE. These are the keys to building a case. Good detectives protect their evidence, write down details about it, and keep track of it. Follow their lead. Make sure to record the details about any evidence you find. You may think you'll be able to remember where you found your clues, but genealogists end up with so many records they could wallpaper an entire room!

GET CLUED IN

- **Rule of thumb.** Provide enough information about where you found your evidence that other genealogists could easily find it on their own. Imagine if you invited friends over to your house but didn't give them your address. Evidence is like that, too. If you don't write down its location, it'll be hard to find—maybe even for you.

- **The basics.** A lot of evidence about your family will be in documents. Write down each document's title, when it was written (and by whom, if you know), and how to find it—either online or in a physical location. Sometimes, you need to include the name of a library or archive, plus any special cataloging information it uses to keep track of documents, such as document numbers, collection names, and file or box numbers.

- **Quality counts.** Details about the evidence itself—not just the information it tells you—help you judge how good the information is. Add notes to help you decide how reliable it is, such as whether your ancestor's name is misspelled, you're not sure an address or date is correct, or the source is somehow suspicious. (You'll learn more about judging the quality of evidence later in this chapter.) Knowing these details also helps when multiple pieces of evidence give you conflicting facts. Consider this example: If your grandmother tells you the date her father died but his tombstone has a different date, which source do you believe?

WRITE IT RIGHT

You've probably seen your parents fill out forms, or maybe you've done it yourself for school or a sports team. Your name goes on one line, your address on another, and so on. It's the same for everyone who fills out the form. Filling out forms may be boring, but it's a way to make sure your school and soccer coach get all the information they need—and that it'll be exactly where they can find it. When genealogists record the details about evidence, they follow a special format, or style, for the same reasons. They write down everything in a certain order to make sure all the information is where they need it and where other genealogists expect it. (Genealogists aren't the only ones who do this. Maybe you've had to use a certain style when writing references for a school report.) Sometimes, it can get a little complicated, because every type of source may have a slightly different format. If you don't want to follow this exact approach, that's OK. But try to include this much information in your records, too.

Check out three different ways to cite evidence:

1. Record of Great-great-great-grandma Anna Lacek's arrival in New York, 1908.

2. Anna Lacek, SS *Noordam* Passenger Manifest, July 11, 1908; stamped page 82, line 3; *Passenger and Crew Lists of Vessels Arriving at New York, 1897–1957* (National Archives Microfilm Publication T715, roll 1122); Records of the Immigration and Naturalization Service, Record Group 85.

3. Anna Lacek, SS *Noordam* Passenger Manifest, July 11, 1908; page 82; *Passenger and Crew Lists of Vessels Arriving at New York, 1897–1957,* National Archives.

Here's another example:

1. Herbert Angel interview, 1973.

2. Sound Recording 64.190: Interview of Herbert Angel by Philip C. Brooks, Jan. 24, Feb. 13, Apr. 5, 1973; National Archives Oral History Project; Records of the National Archives and Records Administration, Record Group 64; National Archives at College Park, College Park, MD.

3. Recorded interview of Herbert Angel, Jan.–April 1973; National Archives Oral History Project, Record Group 64.

As you've probably figured out, Number 1 in both cases doesn't offer enough information to help anyone find the source—or even understand what it is. Number 2 is a professional, grade A, super citation. But if it seems like too much, Number 3 is more of a "Goldilocks approach"—it could be just right for you. It provides enough information to understand the source and find it, perhaps with some extra effort.

WHO, WHAT, WHEN, WHERE

EXPERT TIP

USE THIS FORMAT TO RECORD BASIC DETAILS: INCLUDE FULL NAMES (MAIDEN NAMES FOR WOMEN), WITH NICKNAMES IN QUOTATION MARKS; FOR DATES, ENTER THE DAY FIRST AND SPELL OUT THE MONTH; AND FOR PLACES, LIST CITY, COUNTY, STATE, AND COUNTRY. SO THE ENTRY FOR THE ATHLETE BABE DIDRIKSON ZAHARIAS WOULD BE MILDRED ELLA "BABE" DIDRIKSON, BORN 26 JUNE 1911, IN PORT ARTHUR, JEFFERSON COUNTY, TEXAS, U.S.A.

SUN, WATER, SOIL, AND AIR. THAT'S ALL A TREE NEEDS TO GROW. Your family tree's needs are simple, too. All it needs to grow are a few basic facts: the names of your ancestors and their dates of birth and death. What?! That's all? Where's the challenge in that? Relax, Sherlock. Your detective skills will still be put to the test. Uncovering even your family's basic details takes some super sleuthing. To start your investigation, concentrate on answering these four key questions: who, what, when, and where. That'll help you fill in the basic facts of your family tree.

GET CLUED IN

- **Who.** This is an easy one for your immediate family members. But go back a few generations and throw in some name changes, and it can be a challenge to identify your ancestors. Look for evidence that lists not only your ancestors' names but also their parents and siblings. You'll also need women's maiden names and ancestors' nicknames.

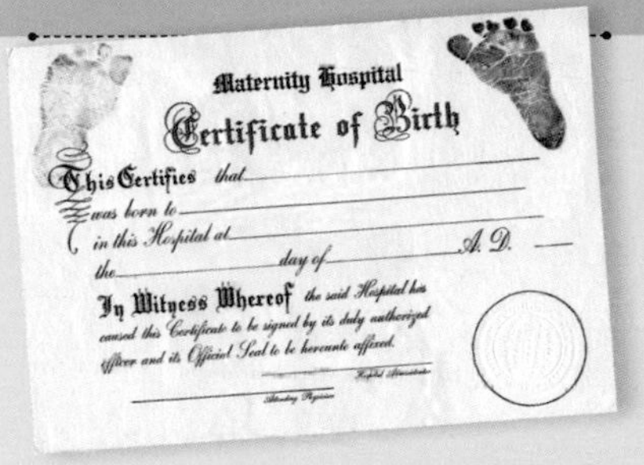

- **What.** Some of the most important events in our lives are births, deaths, and marriages (and divorces). Concentrate on finding out about these, and you'll be able to frame your ancestors' lives.

- **When.** The most important dates to dig up are related to the milestones listed above: birth dates (your ancestors' and their children's), death dates, and marriages. For each ancestor, list birth and death dates, but don't focus only on these dates. You'll also want to look for the birth dates of their children (even if you already know them). They'll help you know you're looking at the right records.

- **Where.** You can trace your ancestors' journeys by discovering where they lived during milestones in their lives. Discovering their whereabouts through time also helps you find and confirm other evidence. But it's a chicken-and-egg thing. You often need to know where your ancestors lived so you can find evidence about their marriages, children's births, and so on.

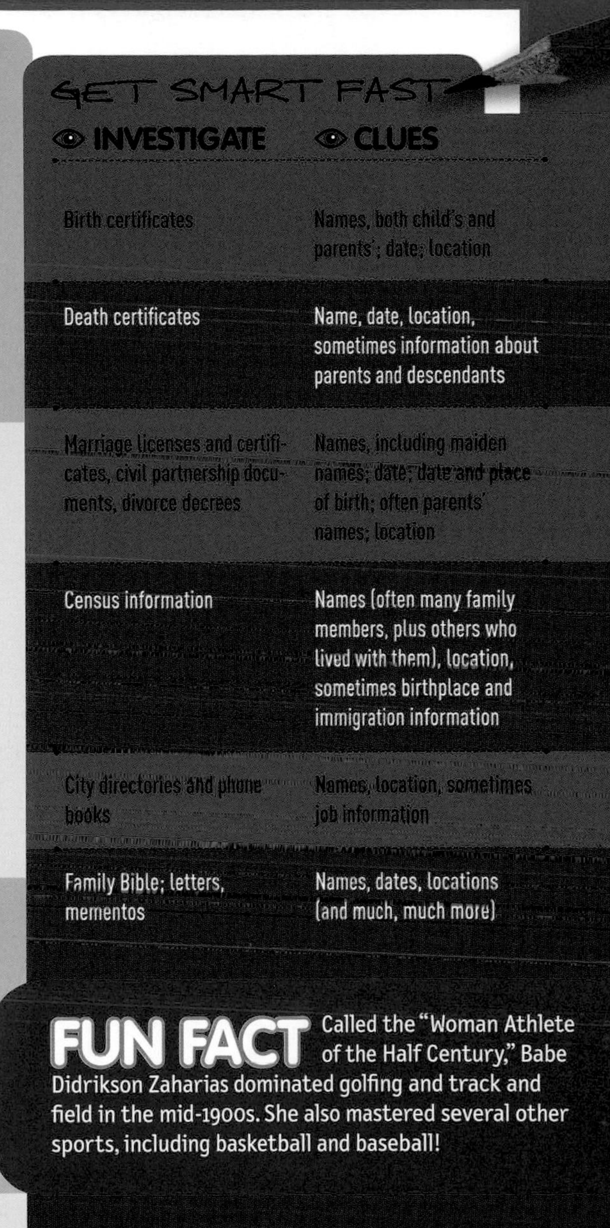

GET SMART FAST

INVESTIGATE	CLUES
Birth certificates	Names, both child's and parents'; date; location
Death certificates	Name, date, location, sometimes information about parents and descendants
Marriage licenses and certificates, civil partnership documents, divorce decrees	Names, including maiden names; date; date and place of birth; often parents' names; location
Census information	Names (often many family members, plus others who lived with them), location, sometimes birthplace and immigration information
City directories and phone books	Names, location, sometimes job information
Family Bible; letters, mementos	Names, dates, locations (and much, much more)

FUN FACT Called the "Woman Athlete of the Half Century," Babe Didrikson Zaharias dominated golfing and track and field in the mid-1900s. She also mastered several other sports, including basketball and baseball!

I, Roger Parmele of the City of New York Nail Manufacturer Do certify that a certain Female Child named Jane — was born on the eighth day of May last past of my Negro Woman Slave named Maria, which Child I retain according to Law —

New York Jany 21 1803

Roger Parmele

WHY AND HOW

WATCHING YOUR TREE BRANCH OUT IS AWESOME, BUT THERE'S A LOT MORE TO LIFE THAN NAMES AND DATES. To add context to your ancestors' lives, answer why they did what they did and how. You can really get a feel for your heritage when you find out what their lives were like: Why did they immigrate to America or elsewhere? How did they make their journey? What were their schools like, and what sort of work did they do? You may not find all that information for each ancestor, but some determined digging will help you fill in a lot of the blanks in your family's past. It's totally worth it. You'll feel connected to lands you've maybe never visited. History will come alive. It'll transform your family tree into a full-fledged family history.

DID YOU KNOW?

If your ancestors immigrated to the United States a century or so ago, they probably didn't come as a family. One person—often the father or oldest son—usually came first and worked to bring the rest over. In the first decade of the 1900s, almost 95 percent of immigrants arriving at Ellis Island were joining family or friends.

GET CLUED IN

- **Why.** Many people move to make better lives for themselves or their families. Your ancestors may have moved to pursue better work opportunities, to try to strike it rich somewhere, or to stake a claim in new lands—or maybe they were forced to move. Wars may have changed their lives, causing them to serve in the military or leave their homes. If any of your ancestors served in the military, moved to new regions, or immigrated, find out what was going on in their lives—or the world—to push them in that direction.

- **How.** Did your ancestors move from the South to the North by train? Did they come to the United States on a ship? Did they head west on a wagon? You may be able to find details about their journey. Or if they had a profession that required specialized training, you may find where they went to school—and learn a bit about what they did outside of study time.

GET SMART FAST

INVESTIGATE	CLUES
Photo albums	Records of important events, including military service and school graduations
Military records	Military service dates and locations; disabilities; military pensions
Immigration papers	Where they came from, when, to where, and how
Land records	Property transfers to children; how the land was used
Diaries, journals, family Bible	Treasure of background information on ancestors' lives
School (including college) yearbooks; programs	Biographical information; details about school activities
Religious documents and publications	Activities; life events, including baptisms, christenings, bar/bat mitzvahs, weddings

RESEARCH ROADBLOCK

WHERE'S PRUSSIA?

SO YOU JUST FOUND OUT YOUR GREAT-GREAT-GRANDFATHER IMMIGRATED TO THE UNITED STATES FROM PRUSSIA. Awesome! You grab your handy world atlas and page through it to find where he came from, but you discover a serious problem. Prussia has disappeared off the face of the Earth. Seriously, it's nowhere. Poof. Gone. Well, that's awkward. Maybe he was from Russia, you think. That occupies a lot of your map's real estate. You check your notes. Nope, there's definitely a "P" at the beginning of the location. Now what do you do?

Don't despair. You just uncovered one of the biggest—and most interesting—challenges confronting genealogical detectives. Borders change over the years. Countries grow, shrink, get divided, or disappear altogether. Some borders are natural—oceans, mountains, rivers, and the like—but most are not. They're drawn by agreement or after conflicts, and they may shift many times depending on who has the upper hand. It's not only land that countries want, but also access to waterways, natural resources, and historically important sites.

Present-day national borders are shown in gray.

The same goes for divisions inside countries. In the United States and many other countries, states are subdivided into counties (or parishes or boroughs). They may change frequently over the years. A state may have started with relatively few, large counties. But as its population increased, it needed more, smaller counties to help administer services. Some counties were divided, others pieced together from parts of neighboring counties. It's possible that one of your ancestors stayed in the same house her whole life but lived in several different counties!

FUN FACT America got its name in the early 1500s, when a German mapmaker named the continent after the Italian explorer Amerigo Vespucci.

GET SMART FAST

INVESTIGATE	CLUES
Atlas of Historical County Boundaries (U.S.), from Chicago's Newberry Library newberry.org/atlas-historical-county-boundaries	Maps and information about county boundaries and how they have changed over time in all 50 U.S. states and the District of Columbia
Atlas of the Historical Geography of the United States, from the University of Richmond dsl.richmond.edu/historicalatlas	A classic historical U.S. atlas that you can click on to see how America has changed over time.
U.S. Geological Survey usgs.gov/products/maps/overview	A national atlas that includes satellite images. Search for and map your ancestors' hometowns.
Bureau of Land Management General Land Office Records glorecords.blm.gov/default.aspx	Land records dating back to 1820, plus images of land plots (survey plats) going back to 1810
Map Warper, from the New York Public Library maps.nypl.org	An interactive map that lets you overlay current maps with historical ones
David Rumsey Map Collection, at the Stanford University Library davidrumsey.com	More than 73,000 historical maps and images, from the 16th through the 21st century. Included are maps from around the world.

HANDLING DISAPPEARING ACTS

All these boundary changes ... It might be tempting just to ignore them and fudge the entry on your family tree. But that would be a grave mistake. Many clues, such as birth, death, and marriage records, are kept by counties or other local jurisdictions, so you need to identify the right governmental office to get these. Besides, it's fun to know exactly where your ancestors lived, so you can trace their steps. Luckily, there are ways to find out.

For U.S. counties, you can look up when a county was created, whether it was cobbled together from other counties, carved out of a larger one, or divided into several others. Great resources are atlases or geographical dictionaries, which list towns and cities along with the names of their counties. Look up a state that interests you, find an index of the counties, then look up a timeline of that county's boundary changes.

For countries, if you can't find similar resources, compare a recent map with a historical map from when your ancestor lived there. Start with a good historical atlas. Look up the name of the town where your ancestor lived in the index/gazetteer portion of the atlas. It'll point you to the specific map in the atlas where the town was (maybe with a page number and other pointers). Once you find the town, note the nearby features: larger cities or towns, natural features, such as rivers, mountains, and lakes. Then match them up on your current map. This will give you the current county or local jurisdiction, where you can look for records.

PROVE IT!

YOUR FRIEND'S LAST NAME IS SWIFT, SO SHE SAYS SHE'S RELATED TO TAYLOR—OBVIOUSLY. Um, excuse me? She's kind of jumping to conclusions, right? You, on the other hand, are a detective. You're going to build a rock solid case about your family connections. No assumptions, no wishful thinking. Just the facts. You need evidence to grow your family tree—and not just any evidence will do. You want to make sure your evidence is accurate and reliable.

HANDLING HEARSAY

If family stories are so unreliable, should you even use them? Yes, yes, yes! Part of the reason you pursue genealogy is to connect with your larger family. What better way to do that than listening to and sharing family stories? The stories also provide valuable clues for your investigation. You'd hate to lose those. Just make sure to confirm all the facts with other evidence. Ever hear the phrase "take it with a grain of salt"? It means you accept something but question its accuracy until it can be confirmed. That's a good approach for family stories. Mine them for clues, but make sure you corroborate the details with other evidence.

GET CLUED IN

- **Reliability.** Evidence is reliable if it tells you what you want to know and is consistent with other pieces of evidence. When detectives find a piece of evidence that confirms a clue they've already found, they call it corroborating evidence. It strengthens their case. When you find multiple pieces of evidence that agree with each other, you'll know you're on the right track. You can use a birth certificate to confirm information in the family Bible or a census record to double-check your great-grandmother's path across the United States.

- **Hearsay.** One of the least reliable types of evidence is hearsay. This is when someone repeats a story he or she heard from someone else. It's secondhand evidence. (Some people even dismiss it as mere rumor.) You can't build your case using hearsay. In fact, it's usually not even allowed in court! Unfortunately for the genealogical detective, some of the best clues are hearsay. They come from family stories, often passed down from generation to generation. They may be the same stories that got you interested in your family history in the first place.

- **Family stories.** Don't get us wrong: Family stories are great. It's just that the details of a story can get a bit twisted each time it's told. People don't always remember events exactly as they happened, especially if they occurred a long time ago. Sometimes they even tweak the facts a bit to make the story more interesting or to keep something private. That makes the genealogist's work more challenging.

ACTIVITY

Play the Phone Game

Still doubt that family stories get twisted over time? Here's a fun—and often ridiculous—way to experience how a story changes when it's passed from person to person.

1. Grab a group of friends or family members—ideally, at least six—and line up or sit in a circle. Space yourselves so you're close enough to whisper to the person next to you without others overhearing what you say.

2. The person who starts the game whispers a sentence or phrase into the ear of the next person—only one time (no repeats). (Tip: Try starting with a sentence that's a little bit silly, like, "The sly red fox borrowed a minivan and drove it to a badger's burrow.")

3. The message gets passed from person to person until it reaches the last person. Each person should try to repeat it as accurately as possible.

4. The last person says the message out loud, and then the first person says what it really was. Chances are, you'll discover that your story took quite a twist!

THE SLY RED FOX BORROWED A...

? @ ! *

FUN FACT The phone game has many names, including grapevine, gossip, secret message, pass the message, the messenger game, broken telephone, whisper down the lane, and don't drink the milk. It's popular around the world.

DOCUMENTARY EVIDENCE

WHEN YOU FIND EVIDENCE THAT'S RECORDED ON PAPER (OR DIGITALLY), YOU'VE FOUND DOCUMENTARY EVIDENCE. It might be an official government document, like a census record, military draft letter, birth or death certificate, property record, or will. Or it may be something less formal, like your great-aunt's diary, a letter from your great-great-grandfather, or notes your mom wrote. If it's written down, it's documentary evidence—and probably one of your most important clues. Genealogical detectives dig into written records for clues about their ancestors' lives. But the records vary a lot in what they tell you—and so does their reliability.

DID YOU KNOW? Have you ever seen "[*sic*]" written in a document? It means that the transcription contains exactly what the original said—mistakes and all. The person who copied the original didn't want to be blamed for the mistake!

GET CLUED IN

- **Reliability.** Documents may be more reliable than hearsay, but some documents are more reliable than others. Examine each piece of evidence and pay attention to these details: What kind it is (government document, personal diary, etc.), what it describes or documents, who created it, when and where it was created, and why it was created. This information—and your critical thinking skills—will help you figure out if it's a good clue. Do you trust the source? Did the source have direct knowledge of the information contained in the document? Was it written at the time instead of much later? Was it intended to be a factual record? The more you answer "yes" to these questions, the better.

- **Originality.** Pay special attention to whether a piece of evidence is a genuine, original document—one created at the time of the event (or soon after), like a marriage certificate. (A scan or photocopy counts as an original, too.) Sometimes you run into documents that were copied from an original, like a friend copying your school notes. These documents are called "derivative" sources because they derive (or take) their information from somewhere else. So what's the problem? When people copy documents, they sometimes make mistakes. A slip of a pencil creates a spelling error; a typo changes a date.

- **Derivatives.** There are different types of derivative sources. Some are transcriptions, copies of entire original documents. Others are extracts, copies of parts of a document—like taking a quote from the document. Still others are abstracts, which are more like descriptions or paraphrases of the original source. If a county clerk keeps a log of marriages—information taken from the marriage license—that's a derivative source. Indexes to documents also are derivative sources. It's best to check the originals to confirm facts.

EXPERT TIP

SOME PEOPLE RECORD ALL THEIR FAMILY'S MILESTONES IN A FAMILY BIBLE. IS IT A PRIMARY OR A SECONDARY SOURCE? HERE'S HOW TO FIND OUT: CHECK THE DATE THE BIBLE WAS PUBLISHED. IF IT WAS A LOT MORE RECENT THAN THE MILESTONES WRITTEN IN ITS PAGES, THE EVENTS WERE RECORDED BY SOMEONE LONG AFTER THEY OCCURRED.

EYEWITNESSES AND OTHERS

Primary sources. Voices from the past. If you find evidence recorded by people who directly participated in or witnessed a past event, you've got genealogical gold. These direct accounts are called primary sources, and they include legal documents, letters, diaries, photographs, interviews, and artifacts from the time, such as souvenirs from events, ticket stubs, and even clothing. If they were recorded at the time of the event or soon after, they're some of the most reliable evidence a detective can find. But beware: Some primary sources, like memoirs and autobiographies, may be written long after an event, when memories may get a bit fuzzy.

Secondary sources. Secondary sources usually were recorded after the event and by someone not directly involved in it, so they may be less reliable. These sources include books, magazine articles, and even genealogies. You may think you've found a treasure if you run across a published genealogy of your family, but remember that it was put together by people whose detective skills you can't judge.

How to tell. It's not always easy to tell the difference between primary and secondary sources. A newspaper article written at the time is a primary source, but one written much later is a secondary source. Here are some questions that will help you figure out what kind of clue you have: Was the person who created the source personally involved in the event? What was the purpose of the source: Did it simply record some information, or did it interpret a previous event? Was the source created at the same time (or soon after) the event or much later?

TEST YOUR DETECTIVE SKILLS

YOU'VE JUST LEARNED ABOUT ORIGINAL AND DERIVATIVE SOURCES. Now it's time to put your knowledge to work. Examine each piece of evidence on these pages and figure out if it's an original or a derivative source. You've got this, Detective.

A. NEW ARRIVALS
An Italian immigrant family arrives at Ellis Island in New York in 1902.

B. HOT TICKET
Did your ancestor live close to the venue listed on this ticket when he or she caught this rock concert?

ANSWERS: A. ORIGINAL. THIS FAMILY'S PHOTO WAS CAPTURED AT THE TIME. B. ORIGINAL. A TICKET STUB IS A FUN SOUVENIR. C. DERIVATIVE. IT'S SERIOUSLY OLD, BUT IT'S A PUBLISHED GENEALOGY. D. ORIGINAL. A CERTIFICATE DOCUMENTS AN EVENT WHEN IT HAPPENED. E. TOUGH CALL, BUT PROBABLY DERIVATIVE. MAGAZINE ARTICLES USUALLY PROVIDE AN ANALYSIS OF EVENTS, NOT EYEWITNESS ACCOUNTS.

C. ROYAL LINEAGE

This fancy drawing, from 1493, traces the genealogy of Charlemagne, a medieval emperor who ruled much of Western Europe from 768 to 814.

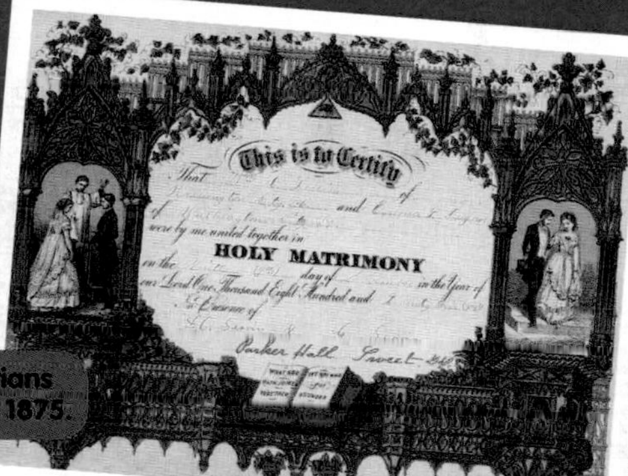

D. WEDDING BELLS

"Holy matrimony" is a term some Christians use for marriage. This certificate is from 1875.

E. COMING TO STAY

Immigration hit the front page of an 1880 Canadian news magazine.

FUN FACT

Ellis Island is located in the Upper New York Bay, which used to have lots of oysters. In fact, long before it became an immigration station, the island was called Little Oyster Island.

CASE FILES
THE FIRST AMERICANS

THE FIRST IMMIGRANTS TO AMERICA WERE THE ANCESTORS OF TODAY'S AMERICAN INDIANS. The details of their journey—exactly how they got here, from where, and when—are still being worked out. But scientists generally believe that the first migrants walked from present-day Siberia to Alaska around 15,000 to 20,000 years ago. Yes, walked. At the time, enough of Earth's water was frozen in massive glaciers to lower sea levels and expose a land bridge connecting the Asian and American continents.

Scientists don't agree on whether the American Indians' ancestors came all at once, maybe over a really long time, or in several migration waves—or if some ancestors came from a different region. American Indians share ancestry with people in Central Asia and Siberia. Some American Indians in South America also share ancestors with Australia's Aboriginal peoples in the southern Pacific.

American Indians' ancestors settled throughout the Americas, paving the way for the cultural and genetic diversity found in today's tribes. Their civilizations thrived on these continents, becoming more diverse and reaching their highest population about 5,000 years ago. But their populations dropped to a low point around 500 years ago, following the arrival of Europeans, who brought disease first, then warfare. As the Europeans/European-Americans colonized the Americas and pushed across the continent, they fought American Indians and forced many off their lands and onto reservations.

RESEARCHING AMERICAN INDIANS ROOTS

Start gathering general materials at home and try early on to identify a tribal affiliation, because the vast majority of American Indian records are grouped by tribe.

For American Indians living in predominantly American Indian areas, special Indian lists (or "schedules") added to the 1900 U.S. census listed tribal affiliations. Elsewhere, the general census simply listed "Indian" under an individual's race. If the 1900 census showed that your ancestor was living in Indian Territory, lands west of the Mississippi River whose boundaries shifted and shrank over the years, eventually becoming part of Oklahoma, check the Dawes Commission Rolls Index, too. The Dawes Rolls, from 1898 to 1906, included members of the Five Civilized Tribes (a term that reflected prejudices at the time)—Cherokees, Creeks, Choctaws, Chickasaws, and Seminoles—who were eligible to receive a piece of land after the Dawes Commission broke up lands held by these tribes. If they lived on reservations, look at the additional census that the Bureau of Indian Affairs took annually on some reservations from 1885 to 1940.

GET SMART FAST

INVESTIGATE	CLUES
AccessGenealogy, a free website with an extensive collection of online resources on American Indian ancestry accessgenealogy.com/native-american	U.S. Indian census rolls; Indian treaties, acts, and agreements; tribal histories; Indian school rosters; newspapers; other references
National Archives and Records Administration (NARA), the official repository for all federal records archives.gov/research/native-americans	Federal records related to American Indians going back to 1774, census records, Bureau of Indian Affairs (BIA) American Indian census records, Dawes Commission Rolls
Cyndi's List, an extensive free genealogical website cyndislist.com/native-american	Links to how-to guides, vital records, census records, maps, history references, genealogical services, message boards, and more
Carolyne's Native American Genealogy Helper, a helpful website started by a journalist and avid genealogist of Cherokee descent nativeamericangenealogy.net	Helpful how-to articles, Native American history, links to Indian census records, tribal-specific census information, Native American legends, stories, and prayers
Oklahoma Historical Society okhistory.org/research/genealogy.php	How-to guide, Dawes Commission Final Rolls, historical background, land records, oral histories
Bureau of Indian Affairs, the official U.S. government agency that deals with American Indian tribes and Alaska Native entities bia.gov	A guide to tracing American Indian & Alaska Native Ancestry (look under the "How do I ..." page), background on U.S.-tribal relations

TOOLS OF THE TRADE

A great detective like you will find lots of clues about your heritage. Seriously, A LOT. How you handle the clues is as important as how you find them. In the next pages, you'll learn the tools of the trade. You'll put together your genealogical detective kit and figure out how to keep track of all that evidence, so it'll be in the right place at the right time. Just like a great detective.

GEAR UP!

CAN YOU IMAGINE a detective interviewing lots of witnesses but not having anything to take notes with? Or gathering up physical evidence—photographs, artifacts, documents—but not having any place to put them? Imagine if she went back to the police station and tossed them in a heap in the corner. Preposterous! You'd never do that, right? Of course not! So get ready to gear up and get organized. We'll walk you through the steps and materials you need to create your detective kit.

EXPERT TIP

BE A COPYCAT. IF YOU COME ACROSS IMPORTANT DOCUMENTS, SUCH AS ORIGINAL BIRTH OR MARRIAGE CERTIFICATES, ASK IF YOU CAN PHOTOCOPY OR SCAN THEM FOR YOUR FILES. PARENTS OR OTHER ADULT FAMILY MEMBERS SHOULD HOLD ON TO THE ORIGINALS FOR SAFEKEEPING.

ROAD TRIPS

You can't find all the clues to your family heritage in your home or online. So the next time you head over the river and through the woods to Grandmother's house, bring along a portable detective kit. As sweet as she is, Grandma probably won't let you make off with all the evidence in her house. But copies and images should be fair game, so bring your recording equipment. Pack your "go bag" with your detective tools: notebook, writing utensils, camera or smartphone, tape recorder, portable scanner (if you have one), flash drive, and small organizing stuff, such as paper clips and sticky notes. Leave most of your files at home, but bring along notes and copies—yes, *copies*—of family group sheets and family trees (also called "pedigree charts"; more on that in a few pages), so you'll remember what information you still need. Use handy plastic or accordion folders to haul your new evidence back home without it getting damaged.

COLLECTING EVIDENCE

- **Notes.** You'll be taking lots of notes. Don't do it on scraps of paper or loose sheets, which can become easily separated from one another. Instead, use a good notebook, such as a spiral notebook, binder, composition book, or journal. For most notes, you can use either a pencil or pen. But if you need to write on the back of a photograph, use a pencil so it doesn't bleed through. Pens with special, archive-quality ink are good options for your files, too.

- **Snapshots.** You'll come across a lot of artifacts that you can't box up, such as souvenirs belonging to cousins or cemetery tombstones. To record this evidence, take a picture of it with a digital camera or smartphone. You'll also want to photograph places that were important to your ancestors, including their homes or the places they grew up.

- **Scans.** If you have access to a scanner, lucky you! Scanning important documents is a great way to hold on to them, as long as you keep track of the electronic files (more on this below). If you have access to a small, portable scanner that you can take along during some of your investigations, even better.

- **Flash drive.** If you plan to keep a lot of files electronically, you may want to have a USB flash drive to back up and transfer computer files.

- **Recordings.** If you interview relatives, it's a great idea to record the interviews. Use an audio recorder app on a smartphone or even a tape recorder. If you prefer to make a video recording, a digital camera or smartphone may be able to handle the task. But beware: Those files are big and can eat up a lot of battery power. No matter how you record an interview, don't rely on technology alone. Take notes in your notebook while you're recording.

- **"Go bag."** Enlist a special bag, like a small backpack, messenger bag, or tote, for carting around your genealogical detective kit when you're on the go. It's fun to get a tote that you can decorate with paint or markers. Where should you keep it when you're not in the field? That's next!

- **Space.** You'll need a special place to store your detective kit and all the evidence you're going to collect. Find a shelf on a bookcase or a corner of your room that you can dedicate to your investigative work.

- **Organizational Tools.** Lots of evidence? Tons of notes? You'll be happy to have paper and binder clips, sticky notes, and rubber bands to help keep it all together. (Tip: Do not use these on valuable documents or photos or for long-term storage. They can harm your evidence.) Your portable detective kit also needs sturdy plastic folders or accordion files for transporting evidence.

PRESERVE THE EVIDENCE

AS YOU GATHER EVIDENCE ABOUT YOUR FAMILY HERITAGE—all those printouts of census records, newspaper clippings, family tree charts, certificates of many kinds, photographs—you will need a reliable place to store it all. (Throwing it in a corner of your room won't work.) There's nothing worse than knowing you have a key piece of evidence but not being able to find it. That happens to genealogists *all the time*. So follow this plan, get organized, and save yourself some grief.

EXPERT TIP

STORE SPECIAL ARTIFACTS AND ORIGINAL EVIDENCE ON THE MAIN FLOORS OF YOUR HOME, WHERE THE TEMPERATURE STAYS PRETTY STEADY ALL YEAR. MANY ATTICS AND BASEMENTS GO THROUGH BIG SWINGS IN TEMPERATURE AND HUMIDITY, WHICH CAN DAMAGE YOUR TREASURES.

DID YOU KNOW?

Long before archival materials and climate-controlled facilities, ancient peoples appealed to divine powers to preserve their writings. In ancient Mesopotamia, the patron god of wisdom, writing, and scribes was Nabu, and texts often referred to him. To note his historical importance, Nabu is sculpted on the doors of the John Adams Building of the Library of Congress in Washington, D.C.

MAKE IT LAST

When you have a valuable piece of evidence, you want it to last for a long time—even long enough for your descendants to see it! Take care of important documents, photographs, and other artifacts by preserving them in archival materials. That may sound like some super-sophisticated, complicated method, but it's not. Archival materials look like regular boxes, envelopes, plastic sheet protectors, pens, and so on, but they're made of materials that won't chemically react with your documents in a way that will damage them, fade them, or turn them yellow. Here's how to tell if you have archival-quality storage materials: Some will simply be labeled "archival," but others will say "acid-free," "lignin-free," "pH-balanced," "pH-neutral," or "passed P.A.T." (photographic activity test). Archival materials are more expensive than the shoeboxes you have sitting around the house, so if you want to save some money, don't use them for photocopies of documents. But they're the best way to take care of old photographs and original documents.

ACTIVITY

Keeping It Together

Flip. Many genealogists like to put their paper evidence in three-ring binders, which they can open like a book and flip through. Each piece of evidence goes in a plastic sheet protector inside the binder, and dividers keep everything in order.

File. If you'd rather let it all hang out, you can organize your evidence using hanging file folders. Manila folders inside the hanging files add to the organization. Even if you don't have a filing cabinet, you can get a nice box that's specially designed for hanging folders.

Pile. If your favorite method of "organization" is to pile things in stacks around your room, have no fear. You can put each pile into an individual box file. Inside each box, try dividing the documents into manila folders or two-pocket folders.

Now that you've decided on your organizational style, get your supplies. If you're a flipper, start with four big binders (or 16 small ones) in four different colors. (Genealogists swear by blue, green, red, and yellow.) You'll want to label them, so look for binders with clear pockets on their spines or use sticker labels on the outside. Pick up a box or two of plastic sheet protectors and some tab dividers for internal organization. If you're a filer, start with a big file box and four hanging files in each of four colors. Get a bunch of manila folders for inside the hanging folders. It's helpful to get them in colors to match the hanging files or get labels you can color code. If you're a piler, start with four big individual box files (or 16 small box files) with matching manila folders or pocket folders for inside.

Going Digital?

Storing files digitally is a great way to organize your evidence. But you can't avoid paper files entirely. You can use smaller binders or file boxes, but you'll still need to file some hard copies of materials, especially any original pieces of evidence you want to keep.

KEEP YOUR FACTS STRAIGHT

YOU'VE GOT THE SUPPLIES TO BE SUPER ORGANIZED. Now it's time to put the plan into action. There are a lot of filing systems you can use—just be consistent. Using colored storage binders, files, or boxes is a great way to stay organized. Putting the organizational system in place takes only a handful of steps.

MASTER OF ORGANIZATION

If you can scan evidence and keep it as a digital file, you'll save a lot more than space. You'll save time, too. You can use an app that lets you add multiple colored "tags" to your files, which you can use to organize and search. For example, you might have a tag for the surname, generation (3G), type of evidence (birth certificate), and so on—whatever you think would be helpful. Go ahead and add a tag if your ancestor had a pet! Organize digital files on your computer or tablet using the same system you use for your paper files.

EXPERT TIP

IF YOU'RE USING HANGING FILES, PUT ALL THE SURNAME TABS ON THE LEFT SIDE OF THE COLORED HANGING FILES. WHEN YOU ADD MANILA FOLDERS FOR INDIVIDUALS, PUT THEIR LABELS ON THE RIGHT. THAT WILL MAKE IT EASIER TO FIND THE FILES YOU WANT.

GET CLUED IN

- **Granddad's blue.** Assign a color to each of your grandparents. All of each grandparent's ancestors will have the same color code. Genealogists often use blue for the paternal grandfather (father's father), green for the paternal grandmother (father's mother), red for the maternal grandfather (mother's father), and yellow for the maternal grandmother (mother's mother). But go with whatever organizing scheme you like. There's no rule that says you even need to use different colors at all—or that you can't use other colors or patterns. Leopard print? Orange polka-dot bow ties? Why not? As long as you're consistent, it'll work.

- **Find your place.** What color will you and your parents have? Well, it depends. Genealogists usually base it on the surname. If your parents have the same last name as their fathers, give them the same color. (Remember to file Mom by her maiden name.) Same goes for you; if you have the same surname as a parent, use that color. But not all families fit that model, so do whatever makes sense to you. It might be the right time to get really creative with your organizing scheme.

- **Line up.** If you're using hanging files, group four of each color in your file box. Label each one with the surname of a great-great-grandparent. (Remember the abbreviations from chapter 1? This would be a 2G-grandparent.) If you don't know one of your 2G-grandparents' names yet, leave it blank. But some will be familiar—like the 2G-grandparent who shares your surname! For big binders and individual box files, use dividers or internal folders to create a space for each great-great-grandparent's surname. Now you'll have 16 organized areas, four in each color.

- **Put yourself first.** When you line up your binders or hang files in your file box, put your surname at the beginning (in the same file as your grandparent with the same last name). For the next color, most genealogists stick with the same side of the family. If your first color files had your paternal grandfather's surname, follow them with the color of your paternal grandmother's surname. Then move to your maternal side. For binders and individual box files, arrange the dividers to do the same thing.

FUN FACT

According to the 2010 census, the 10 most common U.S. surnames are, in order:

Smith, Johnson, Williams, Brown, Jones, Garcia, Miller, Davis, Rodriguez, and Martinez.

Smiths number more than

2.4 million!

- **Divide and conquer.** Label a manila folder for each individual and put it inside the colored hanging file with the same surname. Include the person's name (last name, then first) and birthday on the label. It may be easiest to arrange the internal folders alphabetically, based on the first name, but you can also do it by chronological order, based on each person's birthday. Use internal dividers and pockets inside binders and individual box files the same way. You're ready to file evidence for five generations of your family!

- **Consistency.** When you add evidence to each file, do it in the same order. A good rule of thumb is to follow each ancestor's life timeline, so the birth certificate copy would come first and the death certificate last. If you want to add a file for Great-uncle Joe, put his information in a separate manila folder, but keep it in Grandmother Margaret's file; after all, she was his sister.

- **Know what's inside.** Put a color-coded family pedigree chart in the front file or on the front of each binder. It'll be a quick way to remember who's where in your family tree and files.

PICTURE THIS

FOR A GENEALOGICAL DETECTIVE, FILLING IN THE FAMILY TREE IS LIKE WINNING A GOLD MEDAL. It takes dedicated work to get there, but you'll end up with a prize worth displaying. Family trees can be simple or fancy, but they're always a fun way to see your family heritage.

EXPERT TIP

GO AHEAD AND INCLUDE YOUR **FURRY, FOUR-LEGGED FAMILY MEMBERS** (OR YOUR SCALY, SLIMY, OR FEATHERED FAMILY MEMBERS!) IN YOUR FAMILY TREE. **ADD YOUR ANCESTORS' PETS**, TOO, IF YOU LEARN ABOUT THEM. BUT REMEMBER TO NOTE THE SPECIAL NATURE OF **THE RELATIONSHIP**, SO FUTURE GENEALOGISTS WON'T BE TOO CONFUSED!

DID YOU KNOW?

Your pooch may have a more impressive pedigree than you do! Purebred dogs often have their lineage filed with the American Kennel Club, which also keeps track of awards their ancestors have won. Dogs aren't alone in having this distinction. Horses, cats, cattle, and even zoo animals have registered pedigrees—everyone from aardvarks to zebras!

GET CLUED IN

- **Tree.** A family tree is the most artistic way to display your family. Place yourself on the tree trunk and use the branches for your ancestors. It can take some creativity to work all the relatives in, but the result is totally worth it. There are many ways to do a family tree, but most are based on a family pedigree chart—just turned on its side.

- **Pedigree.** A family pedigree chart, or ancestor chart, may be a genealogical detective's most useful and used record. Unlike a tree that branches up and out, it's a horizontal chart. It begins with you, on the left side of the page, and works back through your direct ancestral lines, with your most distant ancestors on the right side. The chart includes blanks for each person's name and, usually, space for basic information, such as birth, marriage, and death dates and places. The blanks are numbered, from the left and then top to bottom. You're number 1! In a family with one father and mother, the father goes on 2, and the mother on 3, and the numbering continues in that fashion back through the generations. The male ancestors end up with even numbers, and the female ancestors end up with odd numbers.

MIX IT UP

A traditional pedigree or ancestor chart tree is a great way to view your family heritage, but it's not the only way. You might prefer one of these other options, which also show family relations in a fun and interesting way. If you have a family with stepparents, same-sex parents, or a single parent, these charts are easy to adapt to fit your family.

Fan chart. This half-circle chart looks a bit like a proud peacock putting on a show. You're at the center, like you're the peacock's body, and your ancestors spread out like the peacock's tail feathers, with your parents closest to you and your most distant generation farthest from you.

Bow tie. This chart expands in both directions. You're at the center. (As it should be, right?) One parent's ancestors go out to the left, and the other's go out to the right. More than two parents? This may be the chart for you. You can add stepparents easily by adding another line on either side. Another variation is to put biological parents on one side and adoptive parents on the other.

Hourglass. This is a good chart if you want to show someone's ancestors *and* their descendants. The person you're focusing on goes in a box in the middle of the page, and the ancestors branch out on top, as usual. But on the bottom, you add the person's kids, grandkids, and so on.

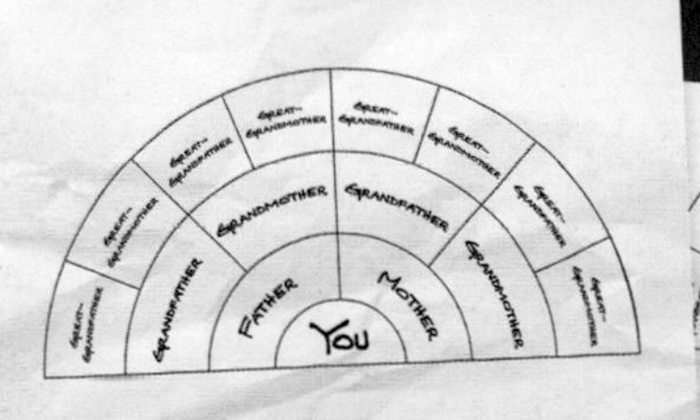

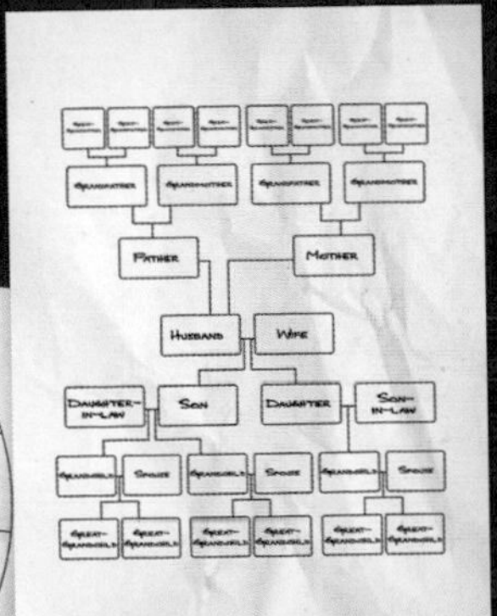

GROUP ACTIVITY

EXPERT TIP

SHOULD YOU NOTE IF SOMEONE IS ADOPTED? IF YOU'RE KEEPING A GENEALOGY FOR MEDICAL PURPOSES, IT MAY BE IMPORTANT TO NOTE IF PEOPLE ARE BIOLOGICALLY RELATED. OTHERWISE, IT MAY ONLY MATTER IF THE ADOPTEE KEEPS UP A RELATIONSHIP WITH HIS OR HER BIRTH PARENTS. TO INCLUDE BIRTH PARENTS IN A GENEALOGY, GIVE THEM THEIR OWN FAMILY GROUP SHEET.

FAMILY TREES AND PEDIGREE CHARTS FOCUS ON YOUR DIRECT ANCESTORS. But good detective work requires you to dig up evidence about other relatives, too. Their lives will tell you lots about your own family heritage. It may be tough to fit all your relatives on your family tree, but you can include them in family group sheets. These handy forms help you organize everything you learn about every member of the family. Along with ancestor charts, they're one of the most valuable tools a genealogical detective can use.

STEPS- AND HALVES AND MORE

How do you handle situations in which parents divorce and get remarried—and maybe have more kids? It seems like a complicated situation for a genealogist, but it's not. Simply create another family group sheet for the new couple and any children they have together. Family group sheets also let you record all kinds of relationships for people who head a family, whether they are married, partners, or friends, or whether they are single.

GET CLUED IN

- **Family.** Instead of focusing on individuals and ancestral lines, a family group sheet focuses on—as the name suggests—one entire family: parents and their children. You'll want to fill one out for every family you investigate.

- **Details.** The forms vary in appearance, but they usually include spaces for each parent's name, occupation(s), birth dates and places, christening dates and places, marriage dates and places, death dates and burial location, names of parents, immigration and naturalization information, military service, and other information. A second page includes spaces to record information about their children: names, gender, birth dates and places, marriage dates and spouses' names, and death dates and places.

- **Sources.** Not all family group sheets have room to include your sources, but don't let that stop you! You can record that important information on a separate sheet; list a source summary for family information, and attach it to the family group sheet.

NATIONAL ARCHIVES

Family Group Sheet

Husband — Date — Place — Occupation(s)

Born / Christened / Died / Buried / Married / Father / Mother

Immigration / Naturalization / Military Service / Cause of Death / Date of Will / Other Marriages

Wife (maiden name) — Date — Place — Occupation(s)

Born / Christened / Died / Buried / Father / Mother

Immigration / Naturalization / Military Service / Cause of Death / Date of Will / Other Marriages

Other Information/Records (ie. Census, Passports, etc...)

National Archives and Records Administration — NARA's website is www.archives.gov — NA Form 14135 (2/13)

Date of first marriage / Name of Spouse — Date of Death/ Cause / Place

* = Direct Ancestor

National Archives and Records Administration — NARA's website is www.archives.gov — NA Form 14135 (2/13)

LOTS OF LOGS

As a good detective, you want to keep track of your investigation's progress. In addition to all the family information you put on charts and family group sheets, keep research logs. You can find special forms online, but a simple notebook will do just fine. Some of the information you should note are sources you consulted, such as books or websites, where they're located, when you looked at them, what kind of information they contained, and other notes—such as whether they were really helpful or totally worthless. What else might be helpful for you to log? People you've interviewed? Locations where various family members lived? Weird terms that genealogists use?

CASE FILES

THE EUROPEANS ARRIVE

THE LONGEST PERIOD OF IMMIGRATION TO AMERICA IN THE MODERN ERA WAS FROM THE 1600s TO THE AMERICAN REVOLUTION IN 1775. A million Europeans set sail on a harrowing two- to three-month journey to the New World in overcrowded, rat-infested ships, where they battled seasickness, disease, and food shortages. Many didn't survive. But the promise of religious freedom, land, and a better life kept them coming.

Pilgrims started this great migration by establishing a colony in Massachusetts in 1620. English Puritans arrived in New England a decade later, followed by more English heading to Virginia. Starting in 1675, a half century of Quaker migration transformed Pennsylvania. Dutch settled in New York's Hudson River Valley, followed by Swedes, who came to the mid-Atlantic region. German immigrants headed mainly to Pennsylvania and New York and later to the South and New England. Immigrants from northern Ireland, northern England, and Scotland pushed into the western colonial frontier.

Many Europeans could not afford the ocean passage, so they sold themselves into indentured servitude, agreeing to work without pay, often for several years. Nearly three-fourths of the English immigrants to Virginia and Maryland and half of the Germans to Pennsylvania probably came over this way. About 60,000 British convicts—typically people whose "crime" was to be poor and out of work—came as indentured servants, often the only arrivals with immigration records.

TRACING EARLY ARRIVALS

If you think your ancestors made it to America before the Revolution, you face some challenges that other genealogical detectives are spared. It's hard tracing your heritage back to colonial America. Official records were scarce back then, so the identities of your ancestor's father and, especially, mother may be very difficult to figure out. And it's even harder to trace your immigrant ancestors' journeys back to where they were born. Before 1820, there was no requirement to keep passenger lists of immigrants sailing to America. But you're not one to shy away from a challenge, right? Knowing where immigrants from different countries settled can help you narrow your search. If you can't find the usual go-to sources, try these genealogical hacks listed to the right.

EXPERT TIP

YOU'VE BEEN DIGGING THROUGH COLONIAL RECORDS, AND, SUDDENLY, THERE IT IS: YOUR LAST NAME! WHEN WE FINALLY FIND A RECORD WITH OUR SURNAME, IT'S TEMPTING TO THINK THAT PERSON IS OUR ANCESTOR, BUT IT MAY BE AN UNRELATED PERSON. BEFORE YOU INK YOUR FAMILY TREE, FIND CORROBORATING EVIDENCE.

GET SMART FAST

INVESTIGATE	CLUES
P. William Filby and Mary Keysor Meyer's Passenger and Immigration Lists Index (Gale Research, 1981–) at major genealogical libraries and online at Ancestry.com (accessed for free through many libraries or for a fee from home)	An index to almost all published lists that document immigration to the United States and Canada, possibly including arrival date, ports of departure and arrival, and family and community members who arrived together
Church and parish records indexed in the International Genealogical Index (IGI), which can be searched online at familysearch.org/search/collection/igi	Baptismal, marriage, and sometimes burial information for colonists, often confirming immigration from Britain and including hometowns of non-British immigrants
Pennsylvania German Pioneers: A Publication of the Original Lists of Arrivals in the Port of Philadelphia from 1727 to 1808, a multivolume collection of colonial passenger arrival lists, reprinted by several publishers, available at large libraries	Records of German immigrants to Pennsylvania—mainly men at least 16 years old—and the ship's name, its captain, ports of departure and arrival, and date of arrival
Probate records (court records created after a person's death that tell what happened to the person's land, belongings, dependents, etc.), many available online at familysearch.org/search	Deceased person's name, spouse's name, children's names, sometimes names of indentured servants
"Pre-1820 Immigration: Tracing Colonial Immigrant Origins," free online lessons by Genealogy Research Associates graonline.com/cgi-bin/gra/getlesson?-1+0+English+education5+graheader+gratrailer	How to find published lists of early immigrants, family histories, genealogical dictionaries, immigrant group publications, church records, court records, land records, probate records, lineage societies

CASE FILES
FORCED MIGRATION

WITH WHITE EUROPEANS CAME ANOTHER GROUP: AFRICANS FORCED TO WORK IN AMERICA. The first African men and women came with European explorers or as indentured servants in the 1500s and early 1600s. But by the 1660s, slaves were brought directly from Africa. The journey, called the Middle Passage, was brutal. Enslaved people were packed into ships' hulls, and rebellions were crushed by armed crewmen. About 12 percent of captives did not make it to the colonies. Those who did were auctioned off and forced to work in awful conditions.

West Africans were brought to the Chesapeake region (Virginia and Maryland), replacing indentured servants on tobacco farms. By the 1730s, more slaves were born there than were brought over.

But in the low country (South Carolina and Georgia), slaves continued to be brought from central Africa to work on rice and indigo plantations. By 1775, people of African ancestry made up 20 percent of the colonies' population; by 1850, most slaves were third- to fifth-generation Americans.

Bringing in slaves became illegal in 1808, but the slave trade continued within America's borders. Southern plantations relied on slave labor. Between 1787 and the beginning of the Civil War in 1861, approximately a million enslaved people were sold "down the river" to cotton and sugar plantations in the South (Alabama, Mississippi, Louisiana). This regional trade affected twice as many people as the earlier trans-atlantic slave trade.

RESEARCHING EARLY AFRICAN-AMERICAN HERITAGE

Researching your African-American heritage can be hard. It can be emotionally difficult to revisit some of the worst aspects of American society—especially when you learn what your ancestors endured. It also can be challenging to find the right evidence, so you'll need your best genealogical detective skills. (Be aware that some of the terms used in old records are offensive.) Make it a goal to trace your heritage back to the 1870 U.S. census. It's the first one taken after the Civil War, which ended in 1865, and the first that lists former slaves by name. If your ancestor was among the many free African Americans, you can go back even further without many problems. But it gets more complicated if your ancestor was enslaved. In that case, you will need to research the slaveowner's records for clues to your ancestor and look for tallies of slaves. First, though, find out everything you can about your ancestors after they were freed. Note their ages and other identifying information, and keep track of siblings and neighbors and places where they lived. These details will help you piece together your ancestors' pasts. It's extra work, but totally worth it. You'll discover the story of strong, resilient ancestors. The sources at right will help you on your journey.

GET SMART FAST

INVESTIGATE	CLUES
Quick Guide to African American Records, FamilySearch familysearch.org/wiki/en/Quick_Guide_to_African_American_Records	Search strategies, links to records, Underground Railroad information, tutorials, and more
Digital Library on American Slavery, University of North Carolina–Greensboro library.uncg.edu/slavery	Names and data on 150,000 individuals, including slaves, free people of color, and slave-owners; runaway slave advertisements published in North Carolina newspapers; slave sale information
Lowcountry Africana, African American Genealogy in South Carolina, Georgia, and Florida lowcountryafricana.com	Plantation records, Freedman's Bureau records, and more related to the heritage of African Americans in the rice-growing areas of South Carolina, Georgia, and northeastern Florida
Unknown No Longer, a Virginia Historical Society database of Virginia slave names unknownnolonger.vahistorical.org	Many types of documents, including court records, Bible entries, deeds of emancipation and more, related to Virginians of African descent
Library of Congress loc.gov	Books, photos, newspapers, oral histories, and much more, many online; search on "African Americans" or related terms to see what exists in this vast collection
Trans-Atlantic Slave Trade Database, a project supported by researchers and universities in the United States and abroad slavevoyages.org	Information on nearly 36,000 slaving voyages that transported 10 million Africans between the 16th and 19th centuries, including ship information, dates, and information about captives

BEGINNING THE INVESTIGATION

You're geared up. You know the techniques. Now it's time to go. The clues to your ancestry are waiting for you—you just have to find them. In this chapter, you'll discover the places to look and the people to interview. Where do you begin your investigation? It may be closer than you think.

THE PRIME SUSPECT: YOU

SO YOU'RE CHOMPING AT THE BIT TO FIND OUT THE JUICY DETAILS of your great-great-grandma Sarah's voyage across the ocean. We totally get it. Uncovering those great stories is why we dig into our past. But hold your horses: Sprinting ahead several generations isn't the way to win this race. It's a surefire way to gallop down the wrong path. With genealogical detective work, you start with yourself and work your way back. Yep, you've got to be a turtle, not a Thoroughbred. Slow and steady wins this race. So start your family tree with the person closest to you—namely, **you!**

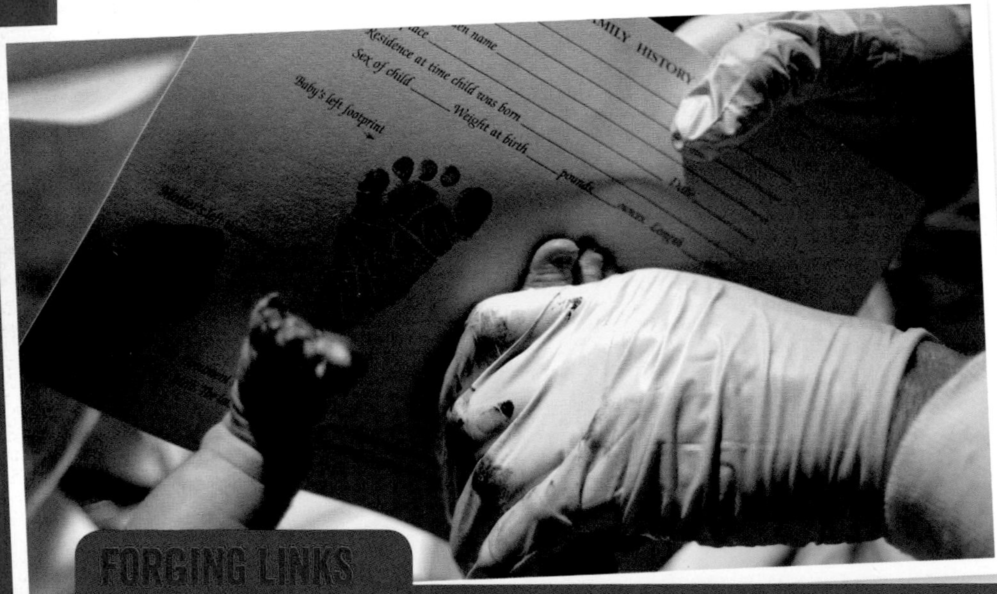

FORGING LINKS

So how exactly do you link generations? Short answer: with documentary evidence. Did you notice that your birth certificate includes your parents' names? Voilà, child linked to parents! Documents that include information about a person's parents, such as their names, ages, and/or places of birth, help you link generations. Lucky for us, some of the most important events in our lives—births, marriages, deaths—include documents with these clues. They let you work your way back through your ancestry, linking each generation to the one that came before it. Brilliant detective work.

GET CLUED IN

- **Trunk.** You begin your investigation by focusing on yourself. You're the trunk of the tree; you support all the branches. So investigate yourself! Get a copy of your birth certificate and note all the information it contains—not only about you but also about your parents. List all the places you've lived and schools you've attended and when. Add any other information that has shaped your life, such as favorite hobbies, sports teams you're on, and instruments you play.

- **Branches.** After you finish with yourself, learn as much about your parents as you can (and as they let you!). Get copies of their birth certificates, marriage license, and other documents. (Make sure you know Mom's maiden name if she changed it.) Find out where they grew up, went to school, lived, and worked. If they've served in the military or been members of churches, synagogues, temples, or mosques, find out where and when. Do the same for your brothers and sisters, then your aunts and uncles. Only then should you go back a generation to your grandparents.

- **Links.** The reason you work your way back generation by generation is to make sure they're connected. You use the information you find out about one generation to link back to the previous generation. If you jump ahead, you risk researching the wrong person. It's a common newbie mistake.

- **Oops.** You've probably heard the phrase, "To err is human ..." We all make mistakes. Even pros have been known to research a family line for years only to discover it was the wrong one. If you start researching the wrong person, no worries. You're in good company.

DID YOU KNOW?

Some people have traced their family trees back to Adam and Eve! Or, at least, they've tried to. Professional genealogists who reviewed the family trees found that most failed to link generations or that some links weren't supported by evidence—and that some even included made-up stuff! But other people have successfully traced their ancestry back to the 500s using documentary evidence. Not bad!

CREATE A TIMELINE OF YOUR LIFE

Now that you've become an expert on yourself, you can be a show-off, too! A great way to display the most important events in your life is by making a timeline. A timeline shows a series of events in the order they happened. It can be vertical or horizontal or even curvy. Grab some art supplies, and see how you can capture the milestones in your life. And, yes, you can do it on a computer, if you really want. Either way, it's a fun and creative way to tell the story of you.

1. BRAINSTORM

Write down every important event you can think of: your baby brother's birth, your first solo bike ride, getting a pet, the first goal you made in soccer, starting school, moving to a new home, making a new best friend—even when you lost your first tooth. Don't forget your birth!

2. BE CHOOSY

Out of your long list of life events, pick the ones that are most important to you.

EXPERT TIP

TO GIVE AN ACCURATE IDEA OF HOW SOON ONE EVENT FOLLOWED ANOTHER, DRAW YOUR TIMELINE TO SCALE. PICK A UNIT OF MEASUREMENT TO REPRESENT A TIME SEGMENT. FOR EXAMPLE, ONE INCH (2.5 CM) COULD EQUAL ONE YEAR. DIVIDE YOUR TIMELINE INTO EQUAL TIME SEGMENTS AND USE A RULER TO PLOT EVENTS IN THE PROPER PLACES.

3. DATE THEM

Make sure you have dates for all your important life events. Ask family members for help if you can't remember them all.

4. ORDER

Arrange your events in the order they happened, from earliest (your birth) to the most recent.

5. NUMBER

Divide your timeline into time periods, such as months or years.

6. PLOT

Figure out where your events fit on the timeline, and fill it in.

7. ART

Add photographs or pictures to make your timeline extra interesting.

8. CONTEXT

If you want, add some important events in your family—or even in the world!—to your timeline. Some people make timelines with their own events on one side and family or world events on the other. It's a great way to make connections.

SUPER SLEUTHING

IT'S NOT LIKE CLUES ARE GOING TO MAGICALLY FALL INTO YOUR LAP, RIGHT? You have to go out and find them. But you don't only need to know *where* to look. You also need to know *how* to look. Use a detective's eye. It's simple. View everything like a piece of evidence you just uncovered, not something you've seen before. Ask yourself what it can tell you about your ancestry. Keep that in mind as you begin to snoop around for clues. You're ready. Now, go for it.

GET CLUED IN

- **Familiar territory.** The first place to investigate? Your home. You can find tons of clues around your own house. And, just like you start your genealogy with yourself, you should first investigate your own home before going anywhere else—including online.

- **Warning, warning!** But, first, a word of caution: Digging through filing cabinets, drawers, attics, and basements can set off alarms—also known as your parents. Before you begin, be sure to get their permission for your investigation. Sometimes it's even helpful to tow them along with you. They may know where a lot of evidence is located, and they can explain clues you find on your own.

- **5 *W's*, 1 *H*.** Remember, the goal of your investigation is to answer questions. When you answer *who, when, what,* and *where*, you'll be able to fill in your family tree. If you can also answer *why* and *how*, you'll understand your ancestors' lives.

MANY MEANINGS

When you use your detective's eye, you'll find clues hidden inside clues. Let's say your family has a fancy red glass souvenir from the 1904 St. Louis World's Fair. It answers a couple of questions about your ancestors: where they were (at least on vacation) and when. But there's a lot more to that special souvenir than those clues. Why, of all the things that your family kept, have they hung on to that souvenir and not some other? If you can answer that question, you'll learn more about the important events of the day and what's important to your family, too.

DID YOU KNOW?

The 1904 St. Louis World's Fair, officially called the Louisiana Purchase Exposition, was the largest world's fair in history. It featured exhibits from more than 50 countries and 43 of the 45 U.S. states at the time and attracted nearly 20 million people during its seven-month run. One of the fair's greatest achievements: making ice-cream cones popular! The fair also served as host to the 1904 Olympic Games—the first Olympics held in the United States—but they were overshadowed by the fair itself.

UNDERCOVER WORK

SOME OF THE BEST PLACES TO FIND IMPORTANT CLUES TO YOUR ANCESTRY ARE HIDDEN. Families keep their most important documents filed away in cabinets—sometimes under lock and key—or even in safety deposit boxes locked in bank vaults. But these aren't the only clues you'll find in hidden places. Attics crammed with boxes of family memorabilia, letters tucked away in old shoe boxes, desk drawers filled with papers—they all hold clues to your past. Make them an early stop on your investigation.

FUN FACT Government documents are called "vital records" in the United States and "civil registration records" in Canada, Great Britain, Mexico, and elsewhere. In some places, the quick way to refer to them is "BMDs"—shorthand for "birth, marriage, and death."

GET CLUED IN

- **Memories.** This is definitely a time to have a parent help your investigation. Yes, you need permission to look into these hidden places, but that's not the only reason you want a parent along. You also can learn so much by going through this evidence together. Don't rush it: Do it when you both have plenty time to explore, so Mom or Dad can talk about what you're examining and share some memories. That's the best part.

- **Milestones.** The official documents that record your family's milestones will help you fill in the blanks on your family tree. These vital records help you find and confirm details of someone's life and also link generations. They answer the who, what, when, and where questions. Some of these are pretty obvious: birth certificates, marriage licenses (and divorce decrees), death certificates. But there are more documents you should look for—and ask about. Try to find religious records for events such as baptisms or bar/bat mitzvahs (or other faith-based ceremonies you practice), land deeds, school and work records, and anything related to immigration or military service.

- **Mail call.** Official records aren't the only documents that will help your investigation. Especially before the days of email, people would write letters to others to share important news in their lives. They might write about important events, such as births, marriages, graduations, or deaths. But that's not all. Sometimes they shared details about vacations, updates about other family members, concerns they had, or just details of their daily lives. These details will give you more insight into their lives and relationships than most other evidence. And some of the clues these old letters hold aren't even in the contents. Keep track of the return address and the dates they were written or postmarked to help track where family members lived over the years. Postcards can even provide images to illustrate their lives and adventures.

LISTS AND MORE

Did Grandma send dozens of Christmas cards every year? Even if you can't track down the cards to check for personal messages, you can still learn a lot about your family from Grandma. Most people who send out Christmas cards keep a list of addresses all in one place. If you can get your hands on Grandma's master list, it'll help you track down lots of relatives. There's a good chance she updated it over the years, so you probably will find old addresses on a handwritten list, too. Many people also hang on to old directories so they don't lose contact with people they've known in the past. For the genealogical detective, these old directories are another great source of evidence. Where's the directory from? Who's in it?

EXPERT TIP

DON'T BE CREEPED OUT BY DEATH CERTIFICATES. IN ADDITION TO THE DETAILS OF A PERSON'S DEATH (WHEN, WHERE, CAUSE), THEY MAY INCLUDE INFORMATION NOT RELATED TO THE PERSON'S DEATH, SUCH AS BIRTH DATE, PARENTS' NAMES, AND OCCUPATION. BUT BE SURE TO DOUBLE-CHECK ITS ACCURACY. REMEMBER, THERE'S NO WAY THE PERSON WHO RECORDED ALL THAT INFORMATION GOT IT STRAIGHT FROM THE SOURCE.

RESEARCH ROADBLOCK

WHAT'S IN A NAME?

A NAME IS HOW YOU RECOGNIZE SOMEONE, RIGHT? OF COURSE, IT IS! Unless it isn't. Dig into your family's history long enough, and you'll discover all sorts of tricky name issues. It's not bad enough that your Irish ancestor's name was Margaret Kelly (there are only a bajillion of them), but sometimes she may have been Maggie Kelley, or Peggy O'Kelly, or even Mairead Queally. And that's assuming you can find her maiden name in the first place! Then there's that family line in which all the sons have the same first name—just like their dad or granddad. How do you make sense of that?

First, remember how surnames (family names) came about—and that they didn't even exist before the Middle Ages. Once the population grew large enough that people needed to differentiate between two people with the same name, they added a byname—a kind of a nickname—based on a person's occupation, father's name, place where they lived, or even appearance or other characteristic. So, instead of four Johns in the same village, now you had John Miller and John Johnson and John Hill and John Longfellow.

FUN FACT In 1664, New Netherland, an American colony settled by the Dutch, was ceded to the British. The British recordkeepers, baffled by Dutch patronymics (see sidebar at right), encouraged the locals to adopt "real" surnames.

DID YOU KNOW?

Think your family's surname was changed at Ellis Island? Many families believe an immigration clerk scribbled down their ancestor's strange-sounding name as best as he could—accidentally changing it. Not true! Ellis Island employed translators, and the clerks read names from passenger lists compiled by ticket sellers who spoke your ancestor's language. So who changed the family name? Your ancestor.

Back then, your ancestors probably couldn't read or write. They had no clue how their names were spelled. Later, when it came time to write their names down, Kelly may have become Kelley and Miller turned into Millar. And even if your more recent ancestors knew how to spell their names, they may have decided to change them. Maybe they lopped off part for simplicity's sake, so von Grimmelshausen became Grimm. Immigrants often changed their names to sound more "American." They may have translated their names to English equivalents, with Schmidt becoming Smith and Bianco turning into White. But not everyone in the same family would make the change, so you might have some ancestors with the original German surname Weber and others who switched to the English equivalent, Weaver. If you keep in mind all the reasons names changed, you'll have more success tracing your ancestry.

But surnames aren't the only problems. Sometimes an ancestor went by a nickname, or multiple nicknames, instead of a given name—or all of the above, depending on the situation. In some families, children may have had two given names, with all the sons or daughters having the same first given name (or a variant of it). People often named children after ancestors, so you'll have Karl turning up generation after generation. Think through possible nicknames, and find out if there are any naming customs in your family or typical of your ethnic or religious heritage.

A NEW GENERATION, A NEW NAME

You may face an extra challenge tracing names if your ancestors used patronymics—names formed from their father's name—instead of surnames as we know them today. Here's how a patronymic works: John has a son, whom he names David. The son would be known as David, son of John, or David Johnson. When David has a son, Peter, he'd be called Peter Davidson. As it turns out, a lot of people run into this problem if they go back far enough, probably to the 18th century or so. If you have Asian, Polynesian, Scandinavian, Slavic, East European, Welsh, or American Indian ancestry, you might fall into this group. Yikes! So how do you even keep these people straight? Try filing these ancestors by location instead of by surname. Back then, people didn't move around as much. Families sometimes lived on the same land for generations.

IS MOM A SHUTTERBUG? IS DAD A SENTIMENTAL PACK RAT? Lucky you! You have gold mines of information in your own home. Families who keep photos and mementos of their lives are a genealogist's dream come true. The information you can gather from these sources can provide basic facts, round out lives, and lead to true breakthroughs in your investigation.

FAMILY HISTORIANS

Chances are, you aren't the only member of your family intrigued by your family's ancestry. One of your relatives may already have compiled a family genealogy or written a personal or family history. Sometimes they're given to family members as gifts or even published and included in library collections. If you find one of these, enjoy reading them—but don't think for a minute that your work is done! You need to treat these books as hearsay evidence. They provide important leads to follow, but you still need to double-check all the facts to make sure they're true.

GET CLUED IN

- **By the book.** Scan your family's bookshelves for important clues. Most families have photo albums. In an ideal world, all the photos would be labeled (in pencil to protect the photo) with the names of the people in them, when the pictures were taken, and where. In the real world, that's seldom the case. But don't let that stop you! Go through a photo album with family members. It's fun, and you can find out a lot about your family's history.

- **School spirit.** A school yearbook definitely includes names and dates. But that's not all. Look through the book to find out what activities your relative was involved in. They may give you clues about what your relative did later in life. Did that 4H member become a farmer?

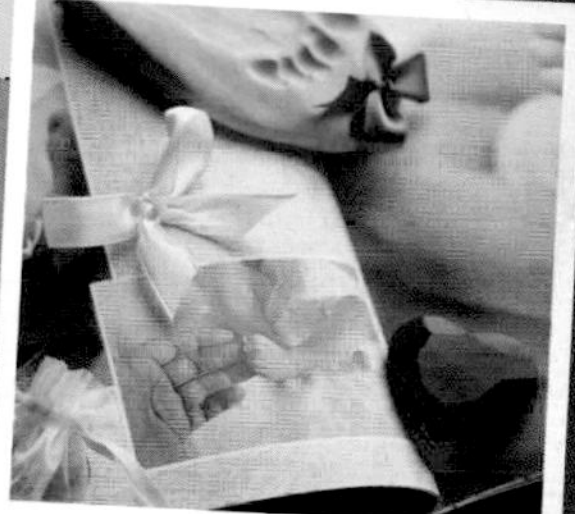

- **Baby steps.** Some families keep baby books that they fill with all sorts of special items, such as photographs, lists of milestones, and snippets of hair. Look for details you need for your tree and also hints of where else to look. A baptism record, for example, may point you to a church where you can find more information about ancestors. Sometimes baby books also include family trees.

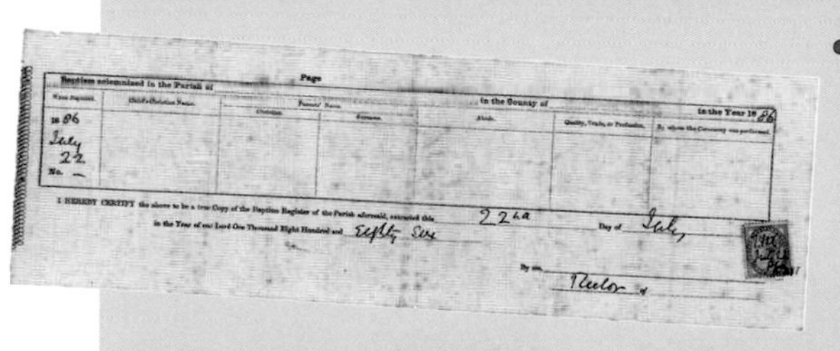

- **In the spotlight.** Almost all our activities have "documents" connected to them. Your family may have kept school programs, church bulletins, or newspaper clippings that mentioned relatives. In addition to the information they contain, other details or clues for other places to look may be discovered if you read between the lines.

- **Treasure trove.** If you're super lucky, a relative collected all these amazing pieces of evidence and put them together in a scrapbook. These decorated albums often record important life events and activities, including vacations, for a person or an entire family. They may include the stories behind photos as well as all kinds of memorabilia.

DID YOU KNOW?

The first school yearbooks didn't include photos! Begun in the 1600s, early yearbooks were scrapbooks for mementos, such as notes, dried flowers, and even locks of hair. Yale University published the first college yearbook in 1806, and a New York high school followed suit in 1845. In the mid-1880s, yearbooks began including students' photos, but teachers were excluded until 1920!

HIDDEN IN PLAIN SIGHT

NO MATTER WHERE IN THE WORLD YOU LIVE, YOU'VE WALKED AROUND YOUR HOME A MILLION TIMES. It's so familiar you could probably make your way around it blindfolded, right? Well, it's time to forget all that, Detective. Look at the things inside your home as if it's the first time you've ever seen them. Check out the special objects sitting on shelves or hanging on walls. What's prominently displayed? What's kept inside special boxes? All these items have stories to tell.

DID YOU KNOW? Home is always a great place to start your investigation. If you are researching your genealogy in a non-English-speaking country, be sure to also consult religious institutions, publications, and documents, which could provide important next steps for your research.

GET CLUED IN

- **Sentimental favorites.** Have you ever wondered about that old, fragile-looking china doll sitting on the shelf? How about that antique toy tractor? People tend to keep toys and other items that bring up a lot of feelings. Take the time to ask about special toys or other memorabilia your parents have. Maybe they belonged to an ancestor, or perhaps they remind your parents of a special time. Learn the stories. They provide clues.

- **Bling.** Ask to check out the family jewelry box. People often engrave special pieces of jewelry, such as rings, with names and dates. If you're really lucky, you'll find an old locket with pictures inside and a message engraved on it. Sometimes old pieces of jewelry can confirm ancestors' names and dates of important life events.

- **Prized possessions.** Are there any trophies or awards displayed? How about framed diplomas or plaques related to an ancestor's profession? Who got these awards? Where did they come from and when? They may give you insights into your relatives' activities and where they lived at different times in their lives.

HOLY PLACES

If you find a Bible on the bookshelf, look through it—especially if it's old or fancy-looking. It might be the family Bible. A lot of families recorded milestones in their Bibles. You may find information about births, marriages, deaths, baptisms, christenings, confirmations, and more. Some families included family trees or tucked other mementos between the Bible's pages. If the Bible is from long ago, it may be the only written record of your ancestors' most important events!

EXPERT TIP

AFTER YOU COMB THROUGH YOUR HOUSE, WIDEN YOUR INVESTIGATION TO THE HOMES OF YOUR GRANDPARENTS, AUNTS, AND UNCLES. BE AWARE THAT SOME OBJECTS AND STORIES MAY BRING UP STRONG EMOTIONS. EVEN IF THE ITEMS ARE EXCITING CLUES, GIVE YOUR RELATIVES ENOUGH TIME TO WORK THROUGH THEIR MEMORIES AT THEIR OWN PACE.

MAKE A TIME CAPSULE

Imagine if you could find an entire treasure chest full of clues about your family's life long ago. You can make that happen! Well, maybe not a real treasure chest, but you can fill a time capsule with treasures to discover in the future. A time capsule is a collection of artifacts that capture what your life is like right now. You seal them inside a container and store it somewhere until a date far in the future, when it's opened to reveal its treasures.

1. DECISIONS, DECISIONS

Who do you want to open your time capsule? A future you? (It's awesome when you're an adult to look back on your childhood.) Your children? Future archaeologists? Complete strangers? Your baby sister when she reaches your age? Once you make that decision, figure out when the capsule should be opened.

HAPPY MOTHER'S DAY!!!

--CONCERT--
LIVE MUSIC
SPECIAL EVENT
FRIDAY 8PM

REGISTERED

AIR MAIL

EXPERT TIP

PUT LETTERS, DRAWINGS, AND PHOTOGRAPHS ON ARCHIVAL-QUALITY PAPER, WHICH LASTS WITHOUT DETERIORATING. COPY NEWSPAPER CLIPPINGS ONTO BETTER PAPER. PLACE PHOTOS INSIDE PROTECTORS THAT HAVE PASSED THE PHOTOGRAPHIC ACTIVITY TEST (P.A.T.). (TIP: PLACE TWO PHOTOS BACK-TO-BACK INSIDE ONE PROTECTOR.) MAKE YOUR CAPSULE'S CONTENTS LAST SO YOU WON'T BE DISAPPOINTED WHEN YOU OPEN IT!

2. CAPSULE

Use a strong, waterproof container that can be sealed really well to keep out water and air. Good choices are stainless steel, aluminum, or copper canisters with secure, long-lasting seals. (Screw caps with gaskets are great.) Polyethylene containers also work, but they should be placed inside a waterproof enclosure if stored outside. It's best to avoid PVC (polyvinyl chloride) if you want the capsule to last a long time, because the chemicals in PVC can damage the capsule's contents over time.

3. TREASURE

What artifacts best capture your life right now? Include photographs of you, your family, friends, neighborhood, pets, even your family car. (Trust us, it'll be hilarious to see it in several decades.) Write a letter describing your life; include your goals for the future and what you think the future will be like. Add a favorite toy. In addition to items that mean a lot to you personally, add some that give an idea of what's happening in the world right now, such as a campaign button from a recent election, a news item, or a current fad.

4. MAKE IT LAST

Leather, wood, and rubber are difficult to store for a long, long time, because they deteriorate and some release gases that harm other contents. It's best not to include them. But if your time capsule wouldn't be complete without your favorite sports ball, you can put it in a special barrier bag that will protect other artifacts. Plastic storage bags made only of polyethylene work. You can also use acid-free tissue paper to separate papers or other artifacts inside the capsule. Don't use tape, staples, rubber bands, or paper clips, which can deteriorate and damage your artifacts. It's best to avoid rubber entirely, and, of course, no batteries or food.

5. PACK

Place your artifacts inside your time capsule carefully. Put the heaviest items on the bottom, so they don't squish the other stuff. If you have any of those packets of silica gel that come with electronics or inside vitamin bottles, throw one into any baggy that contains metal or electronics to help control the moisture level inside. (You can also buy silica packets in hardware or art supply stores.) But don't overload your capsule with them; paper and other organic materials need a little moisture so they don't get brittle. Label the outside of the container with the date the capsule should be opened.

6. STASH IT

Where you place your time capsule will depend on who you want to find it and when. A lot of people think time capsules should be buried, but that's a tough environment for a capsule—and not necessarily the best for the Earth. Besides, you might forget where it is. If you want your own family to open it, place it in the back of a closet or somewhere you store things, like an attic or basement. Some people even make a cool-looking capsule that they put on display! If you want strangers to discover your time capsule in the future, find a hidden place in your home. If a room is renovated, you may be able to hide it inside a wall. If you make a time capsule with friends, family members, or classmates, you may be able to get permission to hide it inside your school, religious institution, or a parent's workplace. Communities sometimes place time capsules in the cornerstones of important new buildings.

INTERVIEWING WITNESSES

EXPERT TIP

TO GET THE MOST OUT OF YOUR INTERVIEWS WITH GRANDMA AND UNCLE BOB, TELL THEM AHEAD OF TIME WHAT YOU WANT TO DISCUSS. BRING A CONVERSATION STARTER, SUCH AS AN OLD PHOTO OF PEOPLE YOU HOPE THEY CAN IDENTIFY. RECORD EVERYTHING, BUT ALSO TAKE NOTES. AND REMEMBER WHAT MOM TAUGHT YOU: DON'T FORGET TO SAY "PLEASE" AND "THANK YOU"!

DOCUMENTS AND ARTIFACTS AREN'T YOUR ONLY SOURCES OF INFORMATION. Think about the people who sit next to you at dinner—or at the Thanksgiving table. Chances are, Grandma or Uncle Bob can provide many clues to your heritage. As a genealogical detective, it's your job to get that information. One of the best ways to do that is to interview your relatives.

WHAT'S LEFT UNSAID

When you're interviewing witnesses, pay attention to more than just their words. A good detective also picks up cues from a witness's body language. When we're happy, excited, or upbeat, we move our arms more, we stand up straighter, and raise our chins. But when we're sad, our bodies really do get a sinking feeling. We drop our arms, hunch our shoulders, and maybe look down. If we feel uncomfortable, we cross our arms in front of ourselves like we're guarding something inside. You want your relatives to feel comfortable talking to you. If you see that you're making someone uncomfortable, make a note of it (it's good to keep track of sensitive issues) and change the subject.

GET CLUED IN

- **Open up.** Interviews don't have to be a game of 20 questions: question, answer, question, answer. Instead, they can be casual conversations. To really encourage the discussion, ask open-ended questions—questions that cannot be answered with "yes" or "no." Try starting your questions with the five *W*'s and the one *H* (who, what, when, where, why, how).

- **Prepare.** Before the interview, figure out what you need to learn from your witness. Go with a list of questions, and make sure you get answers to as many of them as possible. But don't limit yourself to these questions. If the conversation goes elsewhere, follow it. Your relative may know things that are news to you.

- **Key witnesses.** Start by interviewing your parents, and then branch out to grandparents, aunts, uncles, and cousins. As you interview more people, you'll learn more about your family and discover new leads to follow. Some of your relatives may be able to provide documentary evidence that you couldn't find in your own home.

?

Stumped for Questions?

You have a couple of goals for your interview: filling in the blanks on your family tree (and confirming those facts) and rounding out your family history by learning more about their lives. Think about asking questions like these:

- When and where were you born?
- Why was your family living there at that time?
- What was your childhood home like? Was it a house or an apartment? How big was it? Did you have air conditioning?
- Who lived with you in that home? What was the neighborhood like? How far was it from other family members?
- What were your parents' full names, including your mother's maiden name?
- What were your brothers' and sisters' full names? When and where were they born?
- Did you have any pets? What kind, and what were their names?
- What did you like to do when you were young? What kind of games did you play? What was your favorite toy and why?
- Who were your friends? What kinds of things were popular when you were young? What kind of clothes did people wear?
- What's your earliest (or favorite) childhood memory?
- What kind of chores did you do? Which was your favorite, and which was your least favorite? Why?
- Where did you go to school? What was your favorite subject? Favorite teacher? What activities did you participate in?
- What kinds of jobs did you have? Did you like them?
- How did your parents meet? What were they like? What did they do for fun? What kinds of jobs did they have?
- Who are the oldest relatives you remember? What were they like? What do you remember about them?
- Are you named after anyone? Who?
- What was the funniest thing that ever happened to you or your family? The most important thing? The most embarrassing?

CASE FILES
COMING TO BOTH COASTS

DO YOU HAVE IRISH, GERMAN, OR CHINESE HERITAGE? Your ancestors may have arrived in North America in the 1800s. Following a lull during the American Revolution, a big wave of immigration hit both coasts of the United States. The industrial revolution was stripping some people of their traditional livelihoods back home, but work was plentiful in the U.S.

Starting around 1820, immigrants from northern and western Europe—mainly German and Irish—arrived on the East Coast. Many Germans pursued their dreams in the Midwest, buying farms or settling in cities such as St. Louis, Milwaukee, and Cincinnati. The Irish had a harder time. They were fleeing the Great Potato Famine of 1845 to 1849, which led to widespread starvation in Ireland. Many arrived penniless and, without money to travel farther, stayed close to where they had arrived on the East Coast. In the mid-1800s, many Asians, especially Chinese, arrived on the West Coast. Some came hoping to strike it rich in the gold rush (which attracted Europeans, too). Many came to work on the transcontinental railroad.

While the U.S. economy boomed, the immigrants were welcomed. But as the economy slipped into a depression during the 1870s, discrimination rose—especially targeting the Chinese. In 1882, the government passed the Chinese Exclusion Act, banning Chinese workers from coming to America. It was one of the first significant federal laws restricting immigration.

DID YOU KNOW? More Americans claim German ancestry than any other: about 15 percent of the U.S. population, according to the 2000 U.S. census.

RESEARCHING AMERICAN IMMIGRANTS OF THE 1800s

To trace your immigrant ancestors, link back through the generations to find where they first settled. You'll find helpful local records and clues to where they first arrived. New York's Castle Garden was the most common entry, but immigrants also came through Boston, Baltimore, Philadelphia, and New Orleans, as well as smaller ports.

If your ancestors didn't settle near a port city, think about how they likely traveled. Immigrants who arrived in Baltimore and Philadelphia often traveled down the Ohio River to Ohio, Indiana, Kentucky, and nearby states. Those who arrived in New York may have sailed up the Hudson and Mohawk Rivers to Buffalo and across the Great Lakes, settling in western Pennsylvania, northern Ohio, Illinois, Wisconsin, Michigan, Minnesota, or Indiana.

Records of your ancestors' arrivals, such as ship passenger lists, link them to their historical homelands. Look into collections by heritage or country, too. For Chinese-American family research, grave markers often record the place from which men came, and Chinese Exclusion Act records provide lots of details.

GET SMART FAST

INVESTIGATE	CLUES
CastleGarden.org, a project of the Battery Conservancy castlegarden.org	Database on European immigrants arriving in New York, 1820–1892
National Archives–Ethnic Heritage Links archives.gov/research/alic/reference/ethnic-heritage.html	Links to many resources and records from around the world
National Archives–Passenger Lists aad.archives.gov/aad/series-list.jsp?cat=GP44	Records of passengers arriving from various countries
Immigration to the United States, 1789–1930 Harvard University Library ocp.hul.harvard.edu/immigration	Historical materials—books, diaries, biographies, photographs, and much more
Irish Passenger Lists Research Guide by Joe Beine genealogybranches.com/irishpassengerlists/index.html	Information about Irish ship passenger lists and ports of arrival; additional resources
Chinese-American Genealogy guide by Alice Kane americanancestors.org/education/learning-resources/read/chinese-american-guide	Helpful sources, webinar on history of Chinese immigration to the U.S.A., and genealogy tips
Germans to America, edited by Ira Glazier and P. William Filby germanroots.com/gtoa.html	Index of ship passenger arrival records of German immigrants by year

EXPERT TIP

CHINESE NAMES MAY HAVE BEEN CHANGED OVER THE YEARS, SOMETIMES BY ACCIDENT. TRADITIONALLY, A CHINESE SURNAME COMES FIRST, FOLLOWED BY THE GIVEN NAME. BUT AMERICAN RECORDKEEPERS MAY NOT HAVE KNOWN THAT—OR HOW TO TRANSLITERATE CHINESE INTO ENGLISH. IF THAT'S NOT COMPLICATED ENOUGH, CHINESE MEN SOMETIMES ADOPTED ADDITIONAL NAMES RELATED TO THEIR MARRIAGES OR ACHIEVEMENTS.

FINDING CLUES

You've searched your family's attics, dug through drawers of documents, and interviewed witnesses to your family's history. Now it's time to expand your investigation into new areas. An increasing number of clues about your ancestry are online, but not all of them! It's time to whip out your library card.

HIT THE BOOKS

FUN FACT
The Library of Congress, the world's largest library, adds around 12,000 items to its collections daily. It has more than 162 million items on 838 miles (1,349 km) of shelving.

THERE ARE MAGICAL PLACES FILLED WITH EVIDENCE ABOUT YOUR HERITAGE. Maybe you've heard of them. They're called ... drumroll ... libraries. Many libraries and archives have dedicated collections of genealogical materials or terrific collections of family histories and local histories that may shed light on your ancestors' lives. Besides books, libraries have rare manuscripts, special genealogical journals and magazines, and one-of-a-kind materials—evidence you won't find on the Internet. In addition to public libraries and archives, check out the collections of some private libraries and lineage societies. Some libraries are so good that genealogists travel across the country to visit them!

GET CLUED IN

- **Big, small, and specialized.** Large libraries often have impressive genealogical collections covering a broad region and many years. But don't overlook small, local libraries and historical societies! They may have great information about families who lived in their area. Many libraries have a guidebook or pamphlet (hard copy and online) that tells you what kind of materials they have and how to find them. Also, be sure to look through the library's catalog, the database of everything it has in its collection, which often is digitized and available online, even if the materials themselves are not.

- **Your new BFF.** Some of the best resources in libraries and archives aren't dusty old books and microfilm. They're people! Professional librarians and archivists have advanced training in how to do research. They're happy to help you find resources for your genealogical detective work. Some libraries even let you email a question to a librarian. They won't do the research for you, but they'll point you to where you can find the information you need. That kind of help will make you best friends forever!

- **It's too far away!** If you can't travel to a distant library, you may be able to borrow some books through an interlibrary loan service. The distant library will send the book to your local library, if both participate in the service. A word of warning: Reference books, including some genealogy books, often cannot be checked out or obtained through interlibrary loan. But many materials can. The Family History Library sends materials to its branches all over the world. The St. Louis County Library, which obtained the National Genealogical Society's Collection, lends out those 28,000 books, too.

GET SMART FAST

INVESTIGATE	CLUES
Family History Library, Salt Lake City, Utah, the world's largest genealogical library familysearch.org	Huge collection of primary sources, including U.S. federal, state, and county records, family histories, and maps
Library of Congress, Washington, D.C., the world's largest library loc.gov	One of the world's premier collections of U.S. and foreign genealogical collections, with directories, newspapers, photos, and maps
National Archives, Washington, D.C. U.S. government records archives.gov	Census records, military service records, immigration and naturalization records
New York Public Library, New York, New York nypl.org	One of the largest genealogical collections, especially related to New York, Irish, and African-American sources
New England Historic Genealogical Society Research Library, Boston, Massachusetts americanancestors.org	New England records; materials back to the 14th century; extensive Canadian, Irish, and British collections
Mid-Continent Public Library Midwest Genealogy Center, Independence, Missouri mymcpl.org/genealogy	Materials on American slave trade, antebellum South, Southeast, mid-Atlantic, Midwest, and Plains states

EXPERT TIP

YOU CAN SEARCH THE COLLECTIONS OF THOUSANDS OF LIBRARIES AT ONCE AT WORLDCAT.ORG, THE WORLD'S LARGEST NETWORK OF LIBRARY CONTENT. THE SEARCH RESULTS WILL EVEN TELL YOU THE CLOSEST LIBRARY THAT HAS THE INFORMATION YOU WANT. THE POWER OF A SINGLE CLICK!

MAKE YOUR COAT OF ARMS

Coats of arms date back to early medieval Europe. They included symbols—originally worn by a knight over his armor or on his shield—to identify the warrior on the battlefield. In the 17th to 19th centuries, people started to use coats of arms to record their personal or family history. The idea caught on. Soon, all sorts of organizations—such as universities, churches, schools, fraternal societies, and even big corporations—wanted their own coats of arms to symbolize what they were about or to capture their histories. Not everyone has a traditional coat of arms (no matter what some websites tell you!), but it's fun to create one with symbols that have special meanings for you. Here's how:

1. SHIELD

Start by making a shield shape for the center of your design. Decorate the shield with symbols and colors important to you. (Traditionally, warriors used various shield shapes, while non-warriors, including clergy and women, used ovals. But choose any shape that's meaningful to you!) You may get some ideas from these two charts, which include colors and symbols and what they commonly represent.

COLOR	SYMBOLISM
Gold or yellow	Generosity
Silver or white	Peace and sincerity
Red	Strength
Blue	Truth and loyalty
Green	Hope and joy
Purple	Justice and majesty
Orange	Worthy goals or ambition
Maroon	Patience and victory
Black	Faithfulness or grief

SYMBOL	MEANING
Anchor	Hope and steadfastness
Heart	Charity and sincerity
Horseshoe	Good luck
Keys	Guardianship
Lightning bolt	Swiftness and power
Pinecone	Life
Plant	Hope and joy
Star	Excellence, nobility
Sun	Glory and splendor
Sword	Justice and military honor

ANIMAL	SYMBOLISM
Cat	Liberty, vigilance, courage
Dog	Courage, vigilance, loyalty
Dolphin	Swiftness, love
Eagle	Strength, nobility, bravery, alertness
Elephant	Great strength, good luck
Griffin	Valor, death-defying bravery
Horse	Readiness to serve
Lion	Courage, strength, ferocity
Serpent or snake	Wisdom
Unicorn	Extreme courage, virtue, strength

2. SUPPORTERS

Add animals—real or mythical—on both sides of the shield. They support the shield. Animals often are chosen for the different qualities they symbolize, as you can see in the chart.

3. MOTTO

Do you have a favorite saying? (Or how about creating one?) Include it under the shield or above the entire coat of arms. Often, mottoes look like they're on ribbons.

4. HELM

Put a cool-looking helmet or hat on top of your shield.

5. CREST

On top of your fancy helmet or hat, add a decorative plume, animal, or other object to top it all off.

6. MANTLING

If your coat of arms doesn't look fancy enough, add some leaves or other decorations around the top.

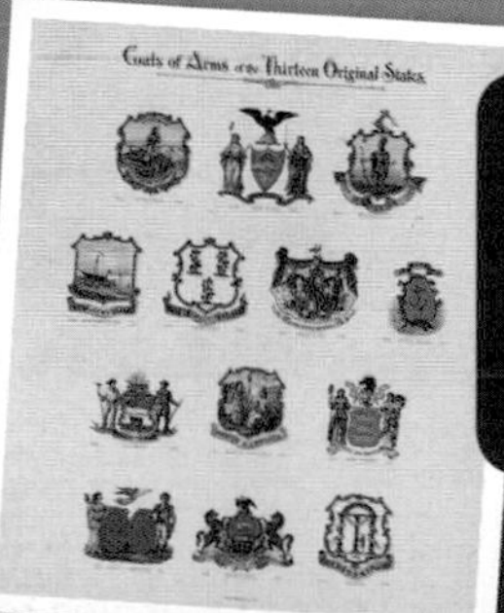

DID YOU KNOW?

The fancy thing most of us call a "coat of arms" has an even fancier name: "heraldic achievement." To be 100 percent correct, the coat of arms is only the design on the shield part, but most people use the term for the whole thing. Similarly, the "family crest" is only the top part of the full heraldic achievement.

COUNT ON COUNTIES

SO WHERE DO YOU GET ALL THE OFFICIAL RECORDS? Washington, D.C.? Probably not. Many useful records—including marriage, birth, death, land, court, probate, and tax records—are recorded at the local or county level. If you can't find them online, you may need to contact or travel to the county courthouse where your ancestor used to live. Woot, woot, road trip! But do your homework before you pack your bags. The date when counties started keeping vital records varies wildly from state to state and even county to county. In some areas, records also have been lost for a variety of reasons.

EXPERT TIP

TO FIND THE LOCAL AUTHORITY THAT HOLDS RECORDS YOU WANT TO SEE, TRY TO SEARCH ONLINE BY THE COUNTY NAME AND TYPE OF RECORD, SUCH AS "BIRTH CERTIFICATES MONTGOMERY COUNTY, ILLINOIS." THE GOVERNMENT'S NATIONAL CENTER FOR HEALTH STATISTICS ALSO PROVIDES LINKS TO FOLLOW AT CDC.GOV/NCHS/W2W/INDEX.HTM

WHILE YOU'RE IN TOWN ...

If you've made a trip to collect files from a county courthouse, chances are you're near another place important to your family: the local cemetery. Stop by and find your ancestors' graves. It's not only a way to feel a personal connection to your past, you'll also be able to verify some important facts about your ancestor. Be sure to take a picture or do a rubbing of the tombstone for your records.

GET CLUED IN

- **Dates.** Though some localities recorded births, marriages, and deaths in the 1600s and 1700s, it wasn't until the early 1900s that local government authorities across the United States consistently kept vital records. Marriage records generally were the first vital records recorded in a county or town.

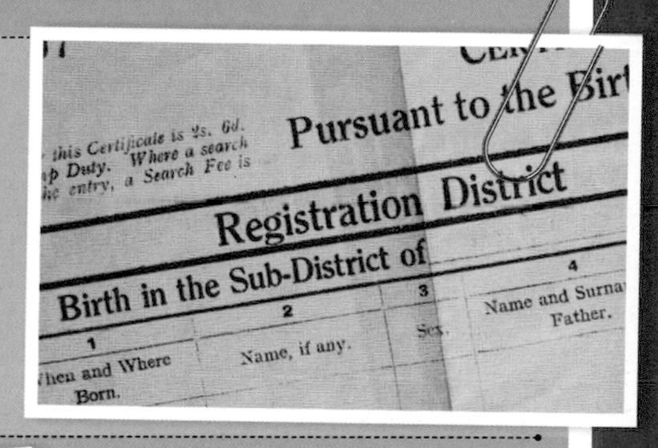

- **Details.** Older birth and death records recorded fewer details than they do today. Early birth records may have included the child's name, gender, date and place of birth, and parents' names. But recent records may include a lot more information, including the hospital's name, parents' birthplace and occupation, mother's marital status, and the number of other children born to the mother.

- **Regions.** Recordkeeping varies by region. New England has good records, some dating as far back as the 1600s. Most states in New England started requiring statewide registration of births, marriages, and deaths between 1841 and 1897. You probably won't find most vital records in the mid-Atlantic states until the mid-1800s, though New Jersey and Delaware recorded marriages starting in the 1660s. In the South, authorities typically recorded marriages as early as the 1700s, but births and deaths were not recorded consistently until the late 1800s or early 1900s. Midwestern states began files of births and deaths as early as the 1860s, though marriages weren't recorded by counties until later. The West varied greatly, with most areas requiring registrations of births and deaths between 1903 and 1920, whereas marriage records go back an additional two or three decades.

DID YOU KNOW?

Disaster strikes sometimes. Important records in many county courthouses have been lost because of floods, fires, tornadoes, rats, leaky water pipes, or simple neglect. During the U.S. Civil War, many courthouses were set ablaze on purpose. You can search online to find out if the courthouses containing your ancestors' records have fallen victim to any of these disasters.

ONE-STOP SHOPPING

AT SOME POINT, YOU'RE GOING TO GO ONLINE. YOU KNOW YOU ARE. Maybe this is the whole reason you wanted to get into genealogy. You've seen the commercials: Some guy types in an ancestor's name and a beautiful family tree leafs out almost right before his eyes! Good detective that you are, you realize it's not that easy. Online investigation requires the same patient approach as any other—starting with yourself and working back, linking generations, and corroborating evidence along the way. That being said, online research is inevitable and a great way to find evidence and tips. Every day, more and more information is put online. Sometimes you have to pay to get to it, but many free sites also offer up a lot of clues.

GET CLUED IN

- **Libraries online.** Online genealogical resources aren't limited to the big websites you see advertised on television. Libraries, archives, and genealogical and historical societies are rapidly digitizing their collections so they can be accessed online. Other "traditional" sites, such as governments, courts, churches and religious offices, schools and universities, and cemeteries are following suit.

- **Mega-sites.** Several websites—both free and subscription—offer a wealth of information in one location. Some are databases of records, some compile other resources in one place, and some provide how-to materials. They're a wealth of information, and they can make your investigation much easier.

- **Just search.** Don't forget to try an Internet search using your favorite web browser. Type in Grandpa's name, or his name and where he went to college. Try several different searches. You may turn up more than you expected, including digitized photographs, newspapers, maps, school yearbooks, and documents.

IF YOU WANT TO TRY A FEE-BASED SUBSCRIPTION SITE, HERE ARE SOME TRICKS. TAKE ADVANTAGE OF FREE TRIAL PERIODS. DO YOUR HOMEWORK FIRST, SO THE TIME YOU SPEND ON THE SITE IS FOCUSED AND NOT SPENT ON RANDOM SEARCHES. MOST IMPORTANT, CHECK IF YOUR LOCAL LIBRARY SUBSCRIBES TO THE SITE (MANY DO). YOU MAY BE ABLE TO GET ON IT FOR FREE!

GET SMART FAST

INVESTIGATE	CLUES
FamilySearch Free site of the Family History Library familysearch.org	Essential site: ability to build and view your family tree, historical records in many collections, message boards and forums, how-to articles
Cyndi's List Free site cyndislist.com	Starting point for finding research resources: compilation of more than 330,000 links to genealogical sites, organized by category and searchable
Ancestry.com Subscription site ancestry.com	Huge databases, easy-to-use family tree building, helpful (free) articles, international sources, especially strong for British Isles and Scandinavia
Find My Past Subscription site findmypast.com	Extensive records, ability to build family tree, especially strong in British Isles
My Heritage Subscription site myheritage.com	Tree-building ability, records, searchable genealogy and history books, ability to search multiple languages
Find a Grave Free site findagrave.com	More than 150 million grave records and other information from around the world
USGenWeb Project Free site usgenweb.org WorldGenWeb Project Free site worldgenweb.org	Volunteer-run sites providing genealogical help and information for every U.S. state and county and every region of the world, respectively
Family Tree Magazine Free and subscription familytreemagazine.com	How-to articles, blogs, templates for family charts and trees, resources for various heritage groups

A LITTLE HELP, PLEASE?

YOU KNOW THERE'S A CRUCIAL PIECE OF EVIDENCE OUT THERE, BUT YOU CAN'T FIND IT. It's either tucked in the musty files of a courthouse far away or missing altogether. Without it, you're not sure you can link the next generation. What do you do? If only you could paste up a bunch of signs around your neighborhood, *"Missing: Great-great-grandpa's wife. Reward, if found."* Hmm, maybe there's a way you can ...

GO SOCIAL

Remember how Mom posted all those pictures of you on social media so your relatives could share in your triumphs: your first tooth, your first sleepover, your piano recital, your science fair project, and on and on? Guess what? The same relatives who liked all those images from afar are now a valuable network. If you're stumped about some piece of your ancestry, ask Mom to post about it and ask those relatives to help.

GET CLUED IN

- **Notices.** Ask a trusted adult to post a notice on an online bulletin board where other genealogical detectives can see it. There's no guarantee someone else will have the answer, but they may—or, at least, they may be able to provide some advice. Message boards and forums are online sites where you can exchange information with others. Some of the best are on *ancestry.com* (go to *ancestry.com/boards*) and *familysearch.org* (*https://familysearch.org/wiki/en/Community_Center*).

- **Friends in need.** You've heard the expression: "A friend in need is a friend indeed." Sometimes your parents can find a volunteer in Great-great-grandpa's hometown who's willing to help in your moment of need. The person may even be willing to run to a cemetery and snap a picture of a tombstone or dig through a courthouse record for you. Sometimes this is done out of a generous spirit, but sometimes it's for a fee—be sure to ask! To find a possible helper, have your parent search for "lookups" on ancestry websites.

- **Get educated.** Chances are you're not the only genealogical detective who's run into your problem. Learn tips and techniques by reading blogs and listening to podcasts, such as Genealogy Gems. Some sites, including the National Archives and Library of Congress, offer webinars focused on genealogy. Many webinars remain available online for watching anytime. Make sure you have a parent's permission to use or to download these online resources.

EXPERT TIP

PROTECT YOUR PRIVACY! MAKE SURE YOU STAY SAFE ONLINE. DON'T EXCHANGE EMAILS WITH ANYONE OR EVER GIVE OUT YOUR PERSONAL INFORMATION WITHOUT YOUR PARENTS' PERMISSION. KEEP PASSWORDS A SECRET. TELL YOUR PARENTS IF SOMEONE ONLINE DOES ANYTHING THAT MAKES YOU UNCOMFORTABLE, AND NEVER AGREE TO MEET AN ONLINE FRIEND IN PERSON. YOU KNEW ALL THIS, RIGHT?

FUN FACT

Sometimes it feels like finding an important clue is magical, like you've been granted a wish out of thin air. Maybe that's why some genealogists call themselves "genies"!

RESEARCH ROADBLOCK

WHY DON'T THE FACTS MATCH UP?

YOUR 4G-GRANDPA FREDERICK WAS BORN IN 1827 IN OHIO, ACCORDING TO THE 1870 CENSUS. Unless it was 1826, and he was actually born in Pennsylvania, like his death certificate says. Then again, maybe it was 1830, and it was Ohio after all, and his name really was spelled Frederic. Groan. And was his wife's name Eliza, Elizabeth ... or Mary? Mary? Where did she come from? Why don't the facts match up? Why is this happening? How are you ever going to fill in your family tree?

Relax, you're not alone. Every genealogical detective digs up evidence that doesn't agree with other evidence. It's more common than you might think. There could be lots of reasons it happens. Some documents, including several years of the census, list ages, but not birth years. Depending on what month your ancestor was born and when the census was taken, it's easy enough to be off a year. Simple subtraction error. But off by three years? It's more likely a mistake. Maybe the census taker thought he knew the information and didn't ask, or maybe your ancestors weren't home when the census taker came, so he asked the kid next door to supply the information. Or perhaps someone fibbed a bit on their age to sound younger. Weird, we know, but it's all happened.

Remember what we said about the reliability of original versus derivative sources? Of course, you do! (Or, if not, go back and sneak another peek at that section in chapter 1, page 31.) Errors are more likely to slip into derivative sources—information taken from other sources. Then there's just sloppiness. You would never do this, but maybe someone else wrote a date like this: 02/03/58. Is that

February 3 or March 2? Who knows? If someone doesn't format the date as 02 March 1958, another conflict slips into your evidence.

Or you could have the totally wrong person. Oh, great. How did the wrong person get into your records? You didn't find someone else's genealogical work and add it to your own without verifying all the information, did you? Maybe you accidentally copied something wrong or your guess about the meaning of an abbreviation wasn't quite right. Or the cause may be even simpler: There are a lot of people with the same name—especially if your ancestor had a common one—and born at pretty much the same time and in the same place. Maybe you got a double.

So, how do you deal with these problems? It's time for a detective's superkeen powers of analysis. After you double-check your notes, look at all the sources that contain the conflicting evidence. Are any of them original documents recorded at the time? Remember, those tend to be more reliable. If they're not, think through when the information was recorded and whether it was close in time to the actual event or much later. (The sooner, the better.) Consider who supplied the information and whether they were in a good position to know all the facts. If you still can't clear up the problem, flag the suspect with a big note or put the person in a "maybe" file. You'll clear up the mystery—eventually.

EXPERT TIP

SAD FACT: IN THE OLD DAYS, MANY CHILDREN DIDN'T SURVIVE TO ADULTHOOD. IF MULTIPLE CHILDREN IN ONE FAMILY HAD THE SAME GIVEN NAME, IT MAY MEAN A CHILD DIED YOUNG AND THE SAME NAME WAS THEN GIVEN TO A YOUNGER SIBLING. PASSING ALONG A NAME WAS A WAY TO HONOR ELDERS. KNOWING THESE TRADITIONS HELPS YOU FIGURE OUT WHAT HAPPENED.

DATE DILEMMAS

If you go back far enough, you may run into date variations caused by different calendars. Most of us use the Gregorian calendar, developed by Pope Gregory XIII in 1582 to improve on its predecessor, the Julian calendar (introduced by Julius Caesar in 45 B.C.E.). The Gregorian calendar tweaked the formula for figuring out a year's length to line up better with the natural cycle of time, including equinoxes and solstices. But it took countries more than three centuries to switch to the new calendar, and it required a big one-time adjustment when they did. Much of Europe changed immediately in 1582, but the United Kingdom and its colonies didn't switch until 1752. To adjust, North America skipped 11 days in September that year. Since the Julian and Gregorian calendars were used in different places at the same time, it's not always clear which one was in effect on a given date—unless it's noted. You may see double dates from 1 January through 25 March 1752. These may be written as 22 February 1731/32 (George Washington's birthday!) or 22 February 1731 O.S. (old style) or 22 February 1732 N.S. (new style). Not everyone adopted the new calendar. Some Eastern Orthodox churches still use the Julian calendar (or a more accurate version of it) to calculate the dates of some holidays.

FUN FACT The anniversary of Russia's "October Revolution" of 1917 is marked every year on *November* 6 to 7. Why? Russia didn't switch from the Julian to the Gregorian calendar until 1918.

MAKE AND KEEP A JOURNAL

Think about all the things you'd like to know about one of your ancestors. Now imagine finding all that information in one place. Almost makes you cry from happiness, right? No? Seriously? OK, imagine that you know nothing about that ancestor—zero, zilch, nada—and have been searching for, like, a billion years. You've gone through every box in your family's house, turned over every rock, and spent so much time digging through obscure books that the librarians made you a birthday cake. Wouldn't it be nice to find one little book that has everything you want to know? *Thought so.*

Don't make your descendants go through what you did. Keep a journal. Fill it with stuff about you—everything from major life events to thoughts about things you like and dislike. Keep adding to it. Remember, who's the best person to record your personal history? You. So get to it; create an original source. In fact, why not create the journal itself? Here's how:

1. GET READY

You'll need several sheets of paper, a sturdy material for covers (the cover of an old notebook, old plastic folder, card stock, cereal box), stuff to decorate the cover (artwork, fabric, stickers, postcards), scissors, glue (optional), a hole punch, a stick about the size of a pencil, and a strong, fat rubber band. (Tip: If you want your journal to last even longer, use archival-quality materials.)

2. SIZE IT

Figure out what size you want your journal to be. If you're using full-size sheets of paper, maybe you want to fold them in half. What size would be handy to have? Make it whatever size you want. No right answers here.

3. FIT IT

Cut the sheets of paper so they're roughly the same size and cut the front and back covers so they're a tiny bit larger.

4. GET FANCY

Decorate your cover any way that you want. Express yourself. Glue may come in handy here.

5. PREP THE FRONT COVER

If your cover is pretty rigid, it'd be a good idea to perform this little operation so it opens more easily: Scratch a straight line down the inside of the cover about an inch (2.5 cm) from the binding edge, so the cover is easy to bend back. An open scissors works better than fingernails for this operation.

6. STACK IT

Sandwich your sheets of paper between the front and back covers.

7. PUNCH HOLES

Punch two holes through all the pages and covers, one hole near the top of the binding edge and another at the bottom. Make sure your stack doesn't shift around a lot while you're doing it! If your journal is thick, you'll need to do a few sheets at a time. Use the top one as a guide to line up all the holes.

8. BIND IT

Stick the tip of your strong, fat rubber band through the top hole, and place your stick through the rubber band on top of the front cover. Loop the rest of the rubber band down along the back cover and poke the other end up through the bottom hole. Scoot the stick so it can slip through that rubber band loop, too. The stick should end up straight along the side of your front cover—very artsy. (If you want a different look, here are two other ways to bind it: Punch three small holes along the edge and use brads. Or staple everything together along the edge and cover the staples with cool-looking duct tape, wrapped from front to back.)

9. WRITE

What to include in your journal: In a nutshell, everything. Sure, put down cool things you've learned about your family. But most of all, write about yourself.

10. WRITE SOME MORE

Journals are best when you keep adding to them.

CASE FILES

HEADING WEST

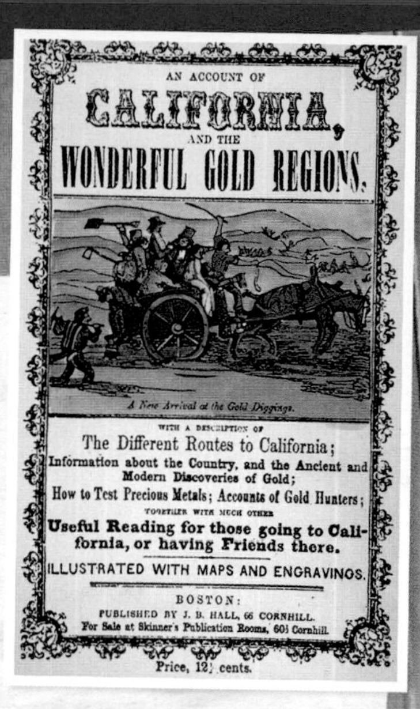

AN ACCOUNT OF

CALIFORNIA,

AND THE

WONDERFUL GOLD REGIONS.

A New Arrival at the Gold Diggings.

WITH A DESCRIPTION OF

The Different Routes to California;

Information about the Country, and the Ancient and Modern Discoveries of Gold;

How to Test Precious Metals; Accounts of Gold Hunters;

TOGETHER WITH MUCH OTHER

Useful Reading for those going to California, or having Friends there.

ILLUSTRATED WITH MAPS AND ENGRAVINGS.

BOSTON:

PUBLISHED BY J. B. HALL, 66 CORNHILL.

For Sale at Skinner's Publication Rooms, 60½ Cornhill.

Price, 12½ cents.

IN THE 1830S AND 1840S, AMERICANS BELIEVED THEIR NATION HAD A RIGHT TO expand across the entire continent—an idea called Manifest Destiny—and by mid-century, it had. But even before that, Americans were on the move. By 1820, about 20 percent of the U.S. population lived outside of the original 13 Colonies. Eventually, hundreds of thousands headed west, often seeking land to farm or, after 1848, hoping to strike it rich in the California gold rush.

From the 1840s through the 1860s, pioneers packed wagons and traveled a grueling four to six months at a walking pace. Many followed the Oregon Trail more than 2,000 miles (3,200 km) from Missouri through the Great Plains and over the Rocky Mountains to Oregon. Some split off and headed south along the California Trail. Others took the shorter Santa Fe Trail from Missouri to New Mexico, while 13,000 Mormons set off from Illinois to Utah. Nearly one in ten pioneers didn't survive—victims of disease, drowning, or accidents. There were some raids by American Indians, but most tribes helped the migrants, often ensuring their survival.

Westward migration boomed after the Civil War. Many migrants were lured by the 1862 Homestead Act, which gave settlers 160 acres (65 ha) of land to farm. The transcontinental railroad, completed in 1869, ended the days of wagon trains but sped up westward moves.

DID YOU KNOW?

After the 1848 discovery of gold in northern California, gold seekers from all over the world rushed to the region in hopes of striking it rich. California's population quadrupled in the 1850s and continued to grow twice as fast as the rest of the United States through the 1870s.

RESEARCHING WESTWARD MIGRATION

When pioneers traveled on wagon trains to the West, recordkeeping was sparse and death rates high. It can be a challenge to find and track your pioneer ancestors. But it's not impossible. Start by using U.S. census records from 1880 back to 1820 to track down your ancestors, identify when they set out and, with luck and determination, find out where they ended up. Census records can be searched online (free at *FamilySearch.org* but also through subscription sites like *Ancestry.com*). To find more information, switch to local sources such as local and county histories that include biographies of early settlers. There aren't comprehensive lists of pioneer settlers, but you can use a variety of sources to identify most of them; some even include the pioneer's place of origin—helpful corroboration. Some sources are shown at right.

GET SMART FAST

INVESTIGATE	CLUES
Paper Trail, an Oregon-California Trails Association website Free to search, but subscription required to see reports paper-trail.org	Searchable index of information in original accounts of overland trail experiences, including names, locations, routes, and more; database includes list of libraries where original documents may be found
Roster of California Pioneers, Native Daughters of the Golden West ndgw.org/PRosterIndex/mainindex.html	Roster of 35,000 pioneers living in California before 1870, with a searchable index
The Oregon Territory and Its Pioneers, by Stephenie Flora oregonpioneers.com/ortrail.htm	Lists of pioneers from a variety of sources, links to research and history sites, and histories of the Oregon Territory and the trails
California State Census of 1852 Note: Although the 1850 federal census covered California, the gold rush caused such a big change in California's population that the state conducted its own census only two years later. familysearch.org/search/collection/1771089	Searchable index of residents of California in 1852; includes names, gender, age, birthplace and estimated year, and citizenship status
Homestead Records, Bureau of Land Management, U.S. Department of the Interior glorecords.blm.gov	Searchable index of land titles given to individuals. Note: Only people who actually were granted a federal land patent are included; nearly 60 percent of homesteaders did not finish the process and aren't listed.

RAPID EXPANSION

From 1803 to 1853, the United States nearly tripled in size. The 1803 Louisiana Purchase doubled the country's area by adding territory that included all or part of 14 current states west of the Mississippi River. In the mid-1800s, the United States gobbled up land all the way to the Pacific Coast. In 1845, it annexed Texas. A year later, it negotiated a treaty with Great Britain to secure the Oregon Territory, which also included present-day Washington State and parts of Montana, Idaho, and Wyoming. After the Mexican-American War, the United States gained much of the Southwest, including California, in 1848 and bought an additional piece of land from Mexico in 1853.

HOT ON THE TRAIL

You're a total detective now. You know how to conduct an investigation, handle clues, and judge good evidence from bad. In the next pages, you'll take a deep dive into the sources that frame a life—the key evidence that answers who, what, and where. So, sharpen your pencils: It's time to hit the trail.

DRAPIER Hugo
2005-
MARTIN Clément
1976-
CURSOL Noémie
1978-
MARTIN Aurélien
1978-
SIMONET Thomas
1980-
MARTIN Caroline
1982-
JACQUET Michaël
1980-
MARTIN Emilie
1986-
MARTIN Justin
1982-
MARTIN Michel
1954-
PLOQUIN Claudine
1951-
MARTIN Bernard
1956-1976
DRAPIER Simone
1934-1935
DRAPIER Serge
1935-
BONNIER Eugénie
1935-1965
MARTIN Simon
1932-
CORBIER Danièle
1938-
MARTIN Christian
1958-
MARTIN Jean
1934-1942
DRAPIER Victor
1908-
MARTIN Germaine
1909-
MARTIN Robert
1936-
MARTIN Augustin
1880-1951
CHARON Mélanie
1882-1964
MARTIN Charles
1910-
ESPIAU Georgette
1912-

VITALLY IMPORTANT!

WHEN GENEALOGICAL DETECTIVES ARE HOT ON THE TRAIL OF AN investigation, they're often discovering details about their ancestors and linking generations using vital records. So what's vital? You'll find different ideas, but a rule of thumb is that vital records—whether for a country or business—are the ones that are essential for the organization to function. For society, that generally means birth certificates, marriage licenses, and death certificates. A lot of people also include the title to their home, diplomas, wills, or other records with long-term significant value, but genealogists focus more on birth, marriage, and death records.

GO BACK

When you want to track down the vital statistics of an ancestor's life, you might be tempted to go in chronological order. It makes sense. But it's actually better to work your way backward. Start by finding death records, then go back to marriage, and, finally, birth records. This may seem upside down, but it's actually good detective work. Just like you build your family tree by working backward from yourself, it's better to work back in an ancestor's life. In addition, it's often easier to find death and marriage records than to find birth records. And when you're lucky enough to find a birth record, the information you got from the death and marriage records will help you know you've found the right person.

GET CLUED IN

- **Think locally.** A lot of vital records are official governmental records, but most weren't created by the U.S. federal government. Local authorities—counties, townships, and states—create birth and death certificates, marriage licenses and divorce decrees, wills, and the like. But when records are tied to events overseas, such as military service or travel abroad, they may be federal records.

- **The good, the bad.** There's little consistency in the content of vital records. Some U.S. states require quite a bit of information, but others don't. Records from the United Kingdom and Canada tend to be on the sparse side. At a minimum, you should find your ancestor's name and the date and place of an event. If you're lucky, you'll also find parents' names, maiden names, and other information. More recent documents tend to include more information.

- **Late or lost.** Some localities started keeping vital records a long time ago—sometimes going back to the 1700s in New England—but other states didn't require them until the 20th century. And many vital records have been destroyed or lost.

- **But, first ...** To find vital records, it's important—probably even essential—that you know where your ancestors lived at various points in their lives. To find that information, dig into censuses.

DID YOU KNOW?

States can use any birth certificate form they want, but in the 1930s most opted to go with a form developed by federal health authorities to improve vital statistics. In 1900, the first standardized form included 33 spaces to fill in. The form developed in 2003 included about 60 types of information—but most could simply be checked off.

MAKING SENSE OF THE CENSUS

EVERY 10 YEARS, THE U.S. CENSUS COUNTS EVERYONE LIVING IN THE UNITED STATES. It gives a snapshot of who we are as a nation, and, if you compare census data over time, where we're going. Because the census is comprehensive, it's the go-to source for genealogical detectives—and with good reason. It lets you find an ancestor at a specific time and place. With that knowledge, your keen detective skills, and a bit of luck, you can track your ancestor across the years and locations. Sometimes census records are the only official government documents you can find for an ancestor, and they're easy to find—the records, that is. Your ancestor may be another matter.

FUN FACT Ancestors aren't the only people you can look up in census records. The 1930 census found aviation pioneer Amelia Earhart staying at the American Women's Association Club Hotel in New York.

GET CLUED IN

- **When and what.** The first U.S. census was taken in 1790. Through 1840, it contained only the names of the heads of household (generally, the father), with other members simply tallied up by age, gender, and race. In 1850, the census started listing all the people in a household—related or not—by name, and, three decades later, it included their relationship to the head of household as well. The census grew more detailed over the years, so by 1940—the most recent year available to the public—it also included such information as a person's occupation, education level, income, and value of house.

- **Where.** In recent years, census documents have been digitized, indexed, and placed online. Most of the online copies include images of the actual census pages, often with the data transcribed as well, plus indexes. You can search them online for free at *FamilySearch.org* but also through subscription sites that may require a fee. *Ancestry.com*, which has a complete set, is available free of charge at National Archives facilities nationwide and through many libraries.

- **Why.** The U.S. Constitution requires the census count. The government isn't just being nosy. Census data are used for several reasons. States use the information to redraw congressional districts, so the seats in the House of Representatives are correctly divvied up. Local communities use the data to figure out where to build roads and schools. Governments rely on census data to figure out taxation and where to provide funding and support.

- **Uh, oh.** Census data can be wrong. The census taker may have gotten the information directly from your ancestor, or he may have gotten it from the kid next door, who didn't really know much. The census taker may have heard some information incorrectly or entered it wrong. Even when the census taker got everything right, your ancestor may have made your investigation more difficult by supplying a nickname instead of a formal name or not remembering where a spouse's parent was born. People who transcribed the information from the census forms to copies also may have made mistakes.

BE A CENSUS PRO

When we talk about the census, we're usually referring to the Population Schedule, the document that identifies people and where they lived. Several detective tricks can help you make the most of these documents.

Go backward. Start with the most recent publicly available census (1940) and work your way back to earlier years.

Be patient. To protect people's privacy, census records are released 72 years after the census was taken, though nationwide data are available within a year after the census. Records through the 1940 census are available, and 1950 records will be released on April 1, 2022. If you really can't wait, you can request your own records or your ancestor's before they're publicly available by filling out a form and paying a fee on the *census.gov* website.

Learn to misspell. Trust us, your ancestors' names will be misspelled at some point. Brainstorm different ways their names—first and last—could be spelled.

Note the neighbors. When you're working through the years, track up to a half dozen of your ancestor's neighbors, too. If you can't find your ancestors one year where you think they should be, look for their neighbors and then read the nearby entries. If your ancestors really are missing, maybe they moved (or they were skipped). Remember, too, that in the past, it was pretty common to marry the boy or girl "next door." That neighbor you've been tracing may turn out to be a relative.

Be flexible. Most of the 1890 census was destroyed in a fire. There have been some attempts to reconstruct it by pulling data from other sources, such as tax records, but you'll probably need to find other evidence for those years. On the other hand, if you're looking for ancestors who lived in 1885 in Colorado, Nebraska, the Dakota Territory, Florida, and the New Mexico Territory, you may be in luck. Those areas were part of a special census, which has been digitized and is available on *Ancestry.com*.

DIGGING DEEPER

EXPERT TIP

IN SOME EARLY CENSUS RECORDS, SUCH AS 1800 AND 1810, THE LISTS WERE COPIED AND REARRANGED ALPHABETICALLY, SO IT'S DIFFICULT TO TRACK NEIGHBORS. HEY, DON'T GROAN: THEY WERE TRYING TO BE THOUGHTFUL.

Take a deep breath: Here comes an avalanche of data. But we're doing it for your own good! The U.S. census varied from decade to decade. Knowing what clues you can find in a given year will help you piece together your ancestors' lives. Remember: Only records through the 1940 census are available; 1950 census records will be released on April 1, 2022.

1790

Name of head of household; number of free white males by age range (16+ or under 16); number of free white females, other free persons, and slaves; state, county, and town of residence

1800 & 1810

Same categories as the 1790 census, but expanded by adding more precise age ranges and age ranges for free white females

1820

Name of head of household; number of free white persons, free "colored" persons, and slaves—all by gender and age range; citizenship status; number of persons working in agriculture, commerce, and manufacturing; county, town, and state of residence

1840

Same categories as the 1830 census, but added ages of military war pensioners and additional disabilities, occupations, education, and literacy

1850

Names of everyone in household; dwelling number; each person's age, gender, and "color"; occupation; value of real estate owned; place of birth; whether married within the year; school attendance; literacy; disabilities; poverty status; convict status; and state, county and town

1860

Same categories as the 1850 census, with addition of the value of personal estates

1880

Similar categories to the 1870 census, but with important addition of specific address (in cities), relationship of each person to head of household, and parents' birthplaces

1890

Similar categories to the 1880 and 1885 censuses, with the addition of ownership and indebtedness of farms and homes; military service in Union Army and Navy

Of note: Most of these records were destroyed by fire, but many records about Union military service survived.

1910

Refined the 1900 census, included disabilities again, and added native language and important information about being a Union or Confederate veteran

1930

Included the same 1920 census questions, added veteran status, and asked if people owned a radio set!

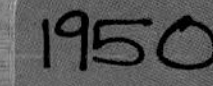

1940

Added to the 1930 census information about highest education level, citizenship of those who were born outside of the United States, residence in 1935, more detailed employment information, income, relationships to veterans, additional questions for women about marriage(s) and children, but no more interest in radios

1950

Similar to 1940 census but with more specificity in some areas, including veteran status

RESEARCH ROADBLOCK

WHAT DOES THAT SAY?

YOU FINALLY FOUND IT: THE KEY DOCUMENT THAT WILL LET YOU LINK YOUR ANCESTORS BACK TO THE 1700s. At least, you think it will. If only you could read it to know for sure. But between the fancy curlicues, ornate flourishes, obscure chicken scratches, and ink splotches, you can't make out a thing it says. It makes you yearn for the precise clarity of the computer-printed copy of your own birth certificate.

The more successful we are as genealogical detectives, the more we run into this problem. At first glance, those old documents look really cool with all their fancy swoops and lines and dots and curls. But they're hard to read, especially if you're not used to looking at that stuff. And then there's the crazy spelling and random capitalization. What's up with that?

Handwriting has changed throughout history. In fact, there were entirely different styles, or scripts, over the centuries. Luckily, learning to decipher those styles is not as difficult as it first looks. (Check out the online guide called "Deciphering Old Handwriting" for tips and examples of dramatically different letters, numbers, and abbreviations.) Once you learn a style, you'll be on your way. At least until the spelling trips you up.

Spelling didn't become standardized until nearly the 1800s. Until that point, there was no "right way" to spell most words. People spelled phonetically, by the sound of the word, and often would spell a word different ways in the same document! Even after spellings became standardized, people may not have had enough education to get everything right.

DID YOU KNOW? Washington, D.C., is missing a J Street. Designer Pierre L'Enfant named east-west streets after the alphabet, but he skipped the letter *J*. For years, Washingtonians wondered whether L'Enfant didn't like John Jay, the nation's first Chief Justice of the United States. Maybe, but it's really 18th-century handwriting that's to blame. *I*'s and *J*'s looked alike and were used interchangeably. Using both would have been confusing!

EXPERT TIP

IF YOU HAVE **TROUBLE UNDERSTANDING** SOME SCRIBBLES, LOOK FOR NEARBY ENTRIES THAT ARE **EASIER TO READ**. STUDY HOW THE LETTERS WERE FORMED, AND TRY **TRACING** THEM IN THE AIR OR COPYING THEM TO GET A FEEL FOR THE **HANDWRITING** STYLE.

It's not just we 21st-century folks who have trouble reading some handwriting. Clerks who had to compile indexes from original documents sometimes couldn't read the originals. *Is that an* R *or a* B *or a* K? They made their best guess—often guessing wrong, leading to a misspelling in the index. As old documents got transcribed and typed up, there was yet another opportunity for errors.

When you run into mangled words, try to pronounce them out loud. You may discover that you know the word after all, and that it was spelled phonetically long ago. Think through letters that resemble each other, and you may be able to figure out the intended spelling. If after all that, you figure out the word, but it still doesn't make sense, remember that words sometimes change meanings over time. That strange old word from long ago may simply be obscure today. A good dictionary will often include archaic (old-fashioned or out-of-date) terms.

SOUNDEX TO THE RESCUE!

The problem of misspelled words—especially when they're names—has plagued genealogists for years, probably centuries. In the early 1900s, two indexing experts, Robert C. Russell and Margaret K. Odell, came up with a solution: a phonetic indexing system that groups together names that sound similar. The system, called Soundex, generates a code for each name based on the sounds of various letter groups. So the names "Stuart" and "Stewart" would have the same Soundex code—as would many misspellings of those names, like "Steward." The federal government has used Soundex for several years of censuses, selected ship passenger arrival lists, some Canadian border crossings, and some naturalization records. *Ancestry.com* and other online genealogical sites use a Soundex search for their huge digitized databases. If you want to see the code for your surname, type your name into a converter at *resources.rootsweb.ancestry.com/cgi-bin/soundexconverter.* In addition to your code, it will show you other surnames that share it.

MORE THAN JUST POPULATION

TO MOST PEOPLE, THE "CENSUS" SIMPLY MEANS THE POPULATION COUNT. But in some years, it also included specialized information that may help your investigation.

SECRET STATE CENSUSES

OK, they're not really secret, but they're so underused, they might as well be. Many (but not all) U.S. states and territories conducted censuses at some point. Some were really serious about it and conducted censuses for many years. Others, not so much. But the state censuses that exist can be great resources for genealogical detectives—especially because they often fell midway between U.S. censuses. Many of them also asked different questions from the federal census, such as prior residences or specific crops grown on the family farm, so they provide evidence that's hard to find elsewhere. To locate state census records, do an Internet search, such as *state census Hawaii* or the like. You'll know you found the right website if its address ends in *.gov*, which is used for government websites. The U.S. Census Bureau's website also includes a list of the state and territorial censuses by location and date. Search for state censuses on the bureau's website, and your search will pull up a link under its history section. Get ready for some super sleuthing!

EXPERT TIP

READING OLD CENSUS RECORDS CAN BE TOUGH. THE CENSUS REFLECTS THE TIME IN WHICH IT WAS TAKEN, AND, LET'S FACE IT, A LOT OF ATTITUDES BACK IN THE OLD DAYS WERE NOT ENLIGHTENED. EVEN THE REGULAR POPULATION CENSUS USES TERMS CONSIDERED OFFENSIVE TODAY. THEY HOLD GREAT CLUES ABOUT YOUR ANCESTRY, THOUGH, SO HANG IN THERE.

GET CLUED IN

- **Slave schedules.** In 1850 and 1860, the census collected information about slavery in states where it existed. These lists included the name of the slaveowner and the number of slaves he owned, including their ages, gender, "color," and disabilities. If a slave was a fugitive, it included that information. It also included how many were released from slavery, or "manumitted." Unfortunately, the names of slaves were rarely listed, but age and gender may provide helpful clues.

- **American Indian censuses.** Two types of federal censuses focused on American Indians. In 1900 and 1910, when census takers came across a Native American while recording census data, they filled out an additional form that included the individual's tribal affiliation, proportion of Indian blood, marriage situation, tax status, dwelling, and, in 1910 only, education. In addition, the Bureau of Indian Affairs recorded an annual census on most Indian reservations from 1885 to 1940. The content varied over the years, but generally included each individual's name (Indian and English), relationship to head of household, age, birth date, gender, marital status, tribal status, and occupation.

- **Mortality schedules.** In 1850, 1860, 1870, 1880, and 1885, census recorders compiled additional lists of people who died during the previous year. The lists included the deceased person's name, gender, age, "color," profession, birthplace, whether the person was widowed, month of death, and cause of death. The 1870 mortality records also included the birthplace of the deceased person's parents. These offer important clues.

- **Farming and manufacturing.** If your ancestors were farmers or industrialists, you may want to dig through special censuses. Starting in 1810, a manufacturing census included the owner's name, type of business, products made, and number of employees. The agriculture schedule, started in 1850, included the owner's name, number of acres farmed, and detailed information about crops and livestock.

FUN FACT Benedict Cumberbatch is the perfect actor to play Sherlock Holmes on the television show *Sherlock*. He's a 16th cousin, twice removed, to Arthur Conan Doyle, who created the legendary detective.

MAKE A BOARD GAME

No one said a genealogical detective can't stop an investigation for some fun and games. And what better way to put your critical thinking skills to the test than to design your own! The options are limited only by your imagination. Before you get out your scissors and markers, think through how your game will be played. Here are some ideas to get you started:

1. HOW DO YOU WIN?

Players need to know what goal they're shooting for. Consider different ways to win a game. Do you have to collect all the key pieces of evidence of an ancestor's history? Is the winner the first person to trace an ancestor's journey from Ireland to Kansas? Maybe you have to fill in a small family tree chart. The choice is yours, but keep the end in mind as you design your game.

2. BRAINSTORM THE PLAY

How do players move around the board? Decide if you're going to use dice, spinners, cards, or other creative ways to move through the game. Decide if players simply move toward the end, or if they have to collect evidence as they go, fill in a family tree, or find real artifacts in your house. What happens to players along the way? Do you want to include challenges they have to perform or obstacles they have to get around? Think of the research roadblocks that genealogists confront.

3. PATH OR FIELD?

Do you want players to move on a path from start to finish? If so, figure out if you want the path to go straight, loop around, split, or some other way. Or maybe you want your players to move into a central field of some sort. If so, what will it look like? A map? You could even combine the two ideas, moving on a path to different rooms or places, like following an investigation from one place you collect evidence to another. Maybe you need to get into a special place to collect clues, but you have to roll a certain number, land on the right square, or pick up a special card to get into the place.

4. LANDING POSITIONS

If you have a path, decide how to break it into landing positions—the little squares, circles, or whatever that make each step along the path. Decide what happens when a player lands on a position. Is it a "safe" place, where they simply move forward on their path? Or maybe a lot of the landing positions have instructions related to the play. It adds excitement when some squares send players to a different place (like back five squares), make players gain or lose items (like key evidence) they've collected along the way, or tell them to draw cards that may help or hurt them.

5. CARDS

Having a stack or two of cards adds an element of chance to the game, and it makes each game a little different, even when you're using the same board. Think about how you could use cards to change a player's position, score, collected evidence, and so on. Will some cards be research roadblocks and others breakthroughs? Decide if the cards are one-time use, something a player may want to keep until an important moment, or something the player can use against a competitor. Maybe they are a way for the player to accumulate wealth or evidence. After you settle all that, decide what kind of information they should contain: Stories? Birth dates? Clues?

6. ROUGH DRAFT

Once you've got the idea for your game, sketch a rough draft of your board design on a scrap piece of paper. Use other scraps to make quick game pieces, cards, and so on.

7. TEST AND TWEAK

Play the game against yourself first and then ask friends or family members to test it with you. After these test runs, make whatever changes you need to clarify rules or make the game more fun. Ask your friends or family members their ideas, too.

FUN FACT

Board games have entertained people for millennia. The game Senet, popular in Egypt as far back as 3100 B.C.E., was found in the tomb of Pharaoh Tutankhamun, or King Tut.

8. MAKE IT

Use sturdy materials, like poster board for the game board and card stock for cards and game tokens. Decorate your board however you like: fancy paper of various colors or designs (scrapbook papers offer a lot of options), markers, colorful duct tape, printouts, stickers, and more. It's probably best not to make your own dice, though!

9. HAVE FUN!

Grab some friends or family members and play your game. They may discover how much fun it is to be a genealogical detective, too!

MEMORY LANE

OVER THE YEARS, A VARIETY OF PRINTED DIRECTORIES HAVE BEEN CREATED TO HELP PEOPLE FIND OTHERS. Long before telephone books, city directories listed the names and addresses of adult (usually male) residents, businesses, houses of worship, and organizations. Specialized professional and business directories listed members of a particular profession or organization and often the services they provided. Even wealthy socialites had their own directory listings, such as the Social Register. In the skillful hands of a genealogical detective, directories can help locate ancestors and information about them. They may include maps and advertisements—maybe some that your ancestor placed!

GET CLUED IN

- **City dwellers.** City directories were often produced yearly, so they are terrific tools for tracking your ancestors' addresses between censuses. Content varied among directories and over the years, but most included information about employment and maybe other family members. Comparing one year to another can tell you if an ancestor changed jobs or even died. (Some specifically listed deaths, while others noted that a person was widowed.) Directories weren't limited to cities. Some counties had them, too.

- **Timebound.** Printed directories often are most useful for researching the late 1800s through the end of the 1900s or a bit beyond. By the late 19th century, populations were large enough that businesses wanted references to help them make contacts. These days, however, online directories and membership rolls have largely replaced printed directories.

- **Cross-references.** Some directories include two ways to look up information. You can look up your ancestors by their name to find their address, or you can look up their address to find who lived nearby. If your relatives moved somewhere, but you don't know where, try contacting their old neighbors. Chances are, they were friends and kept in touch.

- **Finding them.** Fortunately, many city and county directories are being digitized and made available online, often through libraries, historical societies, universities, museums, and online services, such as *FamilySearch.org* and *Ancestry.com.* If you can't find an old directory online, try to look in libraries near where your ancestor lived. If that's far away, contact a reference librarian in your ancestor's old town. If it's a simple request, the librarian may be able to help you. The Online Historical Directories Website provides links to many online directories (*sites.google.com/site/onlinedirectorysite*).

GET SMART FAST

INVESTIGATE	CLUES
City directories books.google.com archive.org familysearch.org	Alphabetical listing of names with addresses, sometimes additional alphabetical listing of streets with people residing at each address
Phone books Look in local libraries and the Library of Congress.	Alphabetical listing of residents' names with addresses, additional listings of businesses and their addresses
Professional, organizational, and academic directories Contact the organizations, professional societies, schools, and libraries.	Specialized listings tailored to a particular profession's or organization's needs; they may be a simple listing of members' names (such as people who went to a particular school or college, members of an engineering society), or include more lengthy biographies.

DID YOU KNOW?

Baltimore may have been the first U.S. city to have a printed directory. The 1752 listing was reprinted eight decades later as *The Following Lists of Families, And Other Persons Residing in the Town of Baltimore, Was Taken in the Year 1752, By a Lady of Respectability.* It's open for debate whether it would be as interesting had it been recorded by a less respectable individual.

WEDDING BELLS

FIRST COMES LOVE, THEN COMES MARRIAGE ... THEN COME CLUES AND LINKS YOU CAN CHERISH! WHAT? That's not how the rhyme goes? No matter: The point is that marriages generate a lot of evidence about your ancestors. Not only can you add that important wedding date to your family tree, but you also can verify spouses' names, find out about parents and relatives, link generations, and get a glimpse of life back in their era. Definitely look for official marriage records—either in counties or churches—but don't stop there. Newspapers can virtually transport you to the ceremony. Raise a toast to the happy couple!

WELCOME TO Fabulous LAS VEGAS NEVADA

DID YOU KNOW? Las Vegas, that city of neon lights, casinos, and Elvis impersonators, is often called the "marriage capital of the world." Marriage licenses in Nevada are easy to get—sometimes taking only minutes—and chapels provide festive and even themed weddings. Couples can get hitched in a fairy-tale garden or on a spaceship!

GET CLUED IN

- **Long tradition.** Marriage records are some of the oldest vital records available. Marriage has always been a public affair, and churches and governments often documented it long before they recorded other life events. The earliest records are found in religious institutions, but town and county authorities recorded marriages pretty routinely by the 1800s and often much earlier in the original 13 Colonies.

- **Go local.** Search for marriage records in the county where your ancestors were married. If you have to guess, try the bride's county first. The easiest way to find the record, if it isn't online, is to look up your ancestor in an index in the county office that keeps marriage records. The index will point you to the location of the marriage record. Contact local religious institutions for the oldest records.

- **Online?** To find out which marriage records are available online, check out *familysearch.org/wiki/en/Summary_of_Marriage_Records_in_the_United_States_by_State.*

- **Read all about it!** Official marriage records aren't the only way to find out about an ancestor's wedding. Marriages were news! When a couple decided to marry, they or their parents often announced it by putting an engagement notice, sometimes with photos, in the local newspaper. (If they were really high society, maybe in a national paper, too.) Newspapers also might have sections listing wedding licenses issued, with the names of the bride and groom, their ages, and maybe other significant information. Sometimes the wedding itself would be covered—with photos and descriptions of the festivities, guests, gowns, and more.

- **Don't forget anniversaries.** Add 25 and 50 years onto your ancestors' wedding date, and you might find newspaper coverage of their silver and gold anniversary parties. It's a great way to track down relatives who came from other towns to share in the celebration.

GET SMART FAST

INVESTIGATE	CLUES
Religious records Look in religious institutions where bride (or groom) lived.	Earliest marriage records and often the only records before the 20th century, with basic information about the couple and marriage date
Civil records Look in county where bride (or groom) has lived. Online: FamilySearch.org – some marriage records, which you can search for free. Ancestry.com has a larger collection of records, which can be searched for a fee or possibly for free from a library that has a subscription.	Marriage registries and "returns" (reports to the civil registrar from the people who performed the marriage ceremony) and civil partnership agreements, with names of couple, date and place of marriage, often name of person who performed the marriage, and maybe couple's residence, names of parents and witnesses, and more; often indexed by both individuals' names
Newspapers Look for recent newspapers online; find many historical newspapers online at Library of Congress at chroniclingamerica.loc.gov/newspapers.	Engagement and wedding announcements; coverage of weddings and anniversaries, with ancestor's name, age, spouse, parents, descriptions of life at the time, names and locations of relatives

EXPERT TIP

IF YOU NEED **CLUES** ABOUT AN **ANCESTOR'S MARRIAGE** IN THE MID-1800s IN THE SOUTH OR NEW ENGLAND, LOOK FOR A **MARRIAGE BANN**. NOT A *BAN*, BUT A *BANN*. THEY'RE TOTALLY DIFFERENT. A BANN WAS AN **ANNOUNCEMENT**—OFTEN IN A CHURCH, BUT SOMETIMES IN TOWN RECORDS—THAT A COUPLE PLANNED TO **GET MARRIED** SOON. IT GAVE PEOPLE THE CHANCE TO OBJECT!

AWW, A BABY

IN THE CHRONOLOGY OF OUR LIVES, OUR BABYHOOD COMES FIRST. So shouldn't birth certificates, too? Nope. These aren't the first records you should try to locate, because they weren't the first vital records that authorities kept. Towns in some areas (thanks, New England!) started keeping birth information long ago, but the practice was not universal until well into the 1900s. To complicate matters even more, different counties within the same state may have started keeping the records at different times. So, should you just give up on birth records? No! They're still gold mines of terrific information.

GET CLUED IN

- **What's where?** Find out when various government offices began to keep official birth records. *FamilySearch.org* provides a list of state links that will answer most of your questions. Find them at *familysearch.org/wiki/en/United_States_Vital_Records.*

- **Inconsistency—again.** Birth certificates come in many formats and contain different details. Some contain the child's name, gender, date of birth, location of birth, and parents' names. Others add information about the child's health, more detailed birth time, ethnic background, and more details about the parents. As with other documents, recent documents tend to include more.

- **Adoption.** When children are adopted—especially if they're infants or very young—their birth certificates may be amended to include the adoptive parents' names. In the United States, the child's original birth certificate, which lists the birth parents, is removed from most files and transferred to the court files that contain the adoption records.

- **Found, but ...** In some states, birth records are kept confidential for 100 years! So, if you do find them, they may not be easy to obtain. You may need to prove that you are a direct descendant of the person whose record you're seeking.

- **Leads.** Birth records may fill in some missing pieces on your family tree, such as a mother's maiden name, the child's and parents' full names, and maybe their religious affiliation. Knowing birth dates and locations also can help you find more evidence about your ancestors, such as land records. Look in newspapers around the birth date for announcements that include even more information.

GET SMART FAST

INVESTIGATE	CLUES
Official birth records Look in county where parents lived. Online: Ancestry websites include some birth records.	Child's name, gender, date and place of birth, parents' names, and maybe hospital's name, parents' birthplaces and occupations, mother's marital status, and number of other children born to the mother
Religious records Look in religious institutions where parents lived.	Child's name, birth date, parents' names, possibly other relatives' names
Newspapers Look for recent newspapers online; find many historical newspapers online at Library of Congress at chroniclingamerica.loc.gov/newspapers.	Birth announcements, possibly with information not contained in official records

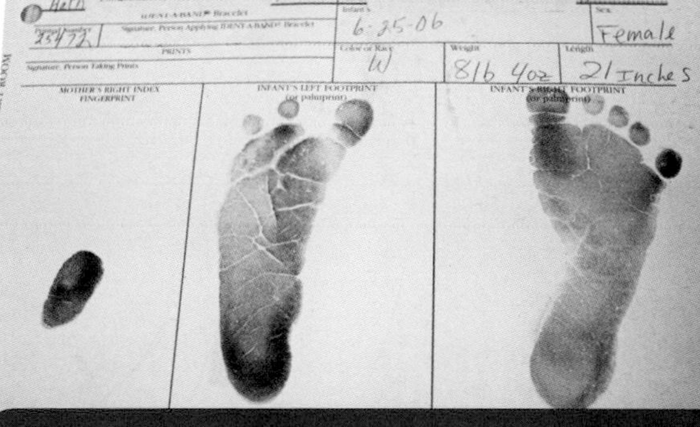

DID YOU KNOW?

Do you have a birth certificate with your footprints from the day you were born? Adorable! But don't try to use it to prove your birthday: It's not your legal birth certificate but rather a souvenir from the hospital. A lot of Americans don't know it's not the real deal and try to use it to as legal proof—like when they want to get a passport. *Oops.*

GETTING DOWN WITH DEATH

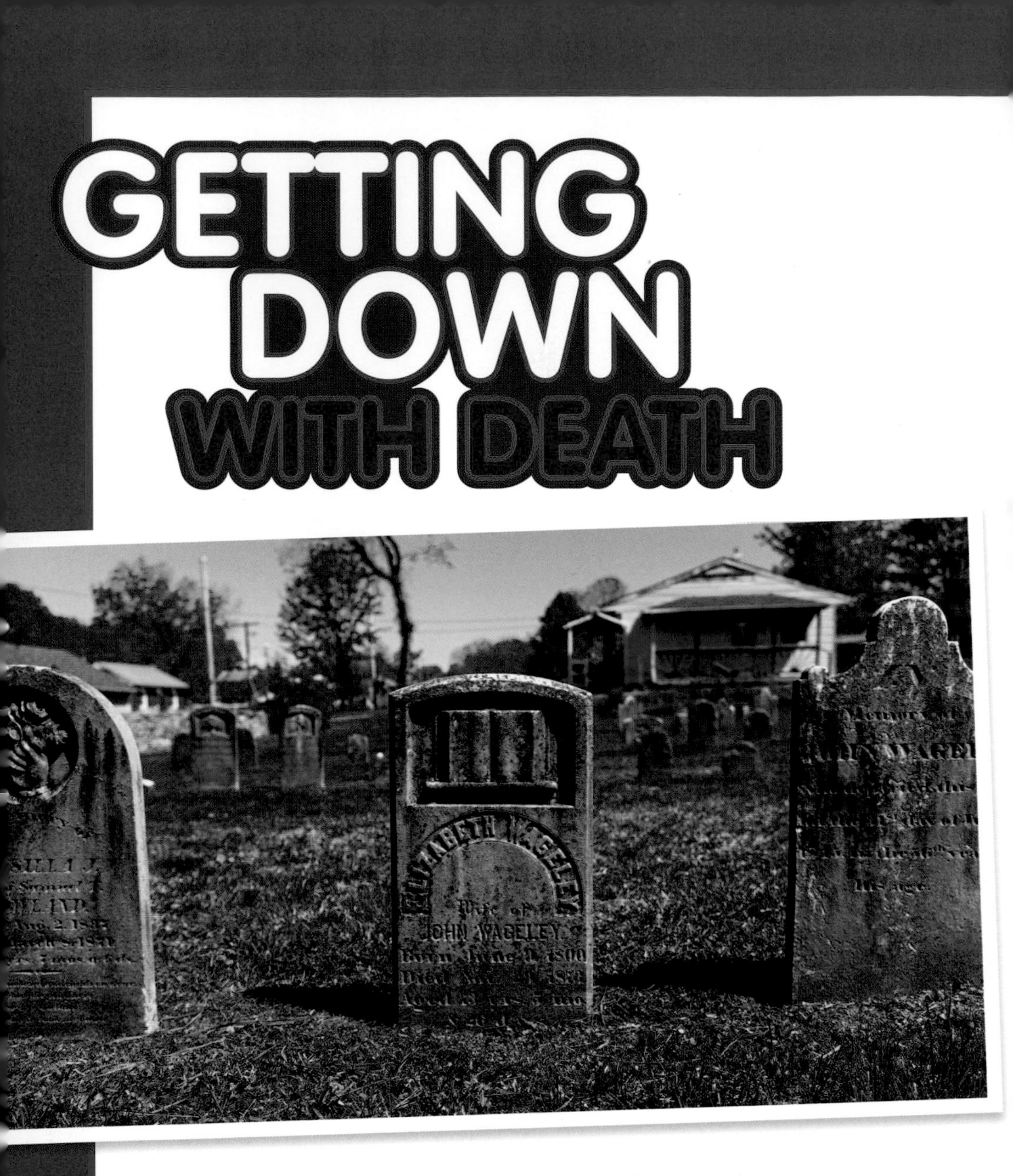

IF YOU THINK DEATH IS KIND OF CREEPY, YOU'LL SOON CHANGE YOUR MIND. For a genealogical detective, death produces valuable evidence. Death records are the most recent documents tied to your ancestors, so they're likely to be really helpful and relatively easy to find. Official records often provide information about a person's birth, spouse, and parents—and often much more. In addition, other documents related to a death, especially obituaries, help paint a fuller picture of your ancestor's life, so you often feel a stronger connection to that family member. Nothing creepy about that!

GET CLUED IN

- **Mixed reliability.** Death certificates include some information—including date, time, and place of death—recorded by an official with firsthand knowledge. But the rest of the information is supplied by an informant, who may not recall all the facts correctly. Make sure you double-check its accuracy.

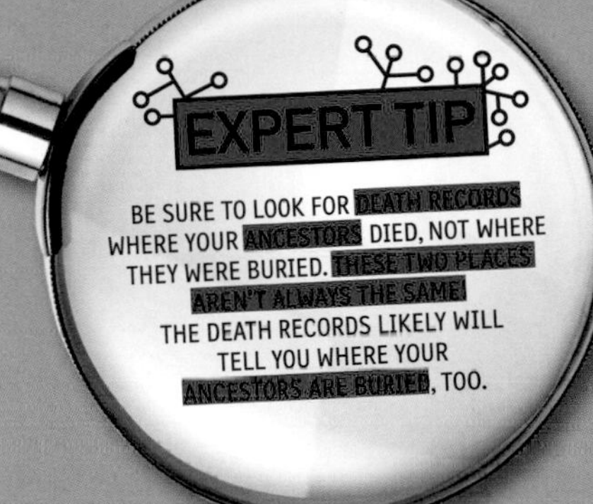

- **Leads.** Because death records often include information about the person's birth date and place, maiden name, year of immigration (if applicable), address, and family members, they can help you find many other pieces of evidence, including immigration records, land deeds, long-lost relatives, and more.

- **Life lessons.** Newspaper obituaries provide more than details about your relative's death. They almost always include information about the individual's life, including professional and other accomplishments, hobbies, religious affiliation, and more. Because obituaries routinely list the person's surviving family members, including where they live, they also link you to other relatives.

GET SMART FAST

INVESTIGATE	CLUES
Death certificates Look where person died. Online: deathindexes.com includes links to sites with online death indexes listed by state and counties; ancestry websites include some death records.	Name, date, and place of death; possibly age, birth date, race, residence, cause of death, burial information, religious affiliation, spouse, parents, name of informant (person who provided information—often a relative)
Religious records Look in religious institutions where person was a member.	Basic information about deceased relative, perhaps family members
Newspapers Look for recent newspapers online; find many historical newspapers online at Library of Congress at chroniclingamerica.loc.gov/newspapers.	Obituaries with information about person's life, profession, education, hobbies, family members, and where they live
Grave markers Online services, such as Find A Grave and BillionGraves, may include listing of grave location and photograph of marker.	Birth and death dates, significant location

DEATHS, MEMO

DEATHS

START GROWING YOUR FAMILY TREE

If you've been digging into your past, it's time to plant and shape your family tree. Your ancestors' names, birth dates, and death dates are all you need to grow it. But, like a good gardener, you can shape it in many ways. At a minimum, you'll have an impressive chart to show for your work. Or you may have a full-grown family tree worth framing. Get out the art supplies; let's see if you can make something as lovely as a tree.

1. GATHER YOUR DATA

If you haven't already, fill out a family pedigree chart with at least two to three generations of your family. Remember, it begins with you on the left and works back to the right, adding each generation of ancestors. Need a little refresher on what that chart is? Check back in chapter 2, page 45, and then come right back. No worries; we'll wait. ... *la de da de da* ...

2. STAND IT UP

Give your pedigree chart a 90-degree turn to the left, so you're at the bottom—like a strong trunk—and your ancestors are branching out over you. That's your inspiration, but you're going to get much fancier.

3. CREATE A TREE

Draw a cool-looking tree. (Spoiler alert: You're going to be on the trunk, and your ancestors will be on the branches. So leave room for the whole happy family, plus pictures.) Make your tree as realistic or abstract as you want. Into impressionism? Go for it. Prefer the stick-figure approach? We're sure you can make it work. Take some time and have some fun.

4. BECOME THE TREE

Put yourself and your family into the tree. Remember: You're the strong trunk at the bottom. The entire tree depends on you. *(No pressure.)* The first set of branches up belong to your parents. The ones that branch off from them are your grandparents. And, yes, of course, if you have brothers and sisters, branch them off your trunk—you know, like little twigs. And don't forget your pets.

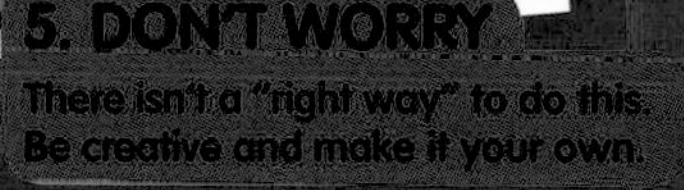

5. DON'T WORRY

There isn't a "right way" to do this. Be creative and make it your own.

6. ADD VISUALS

A family tree really bears fruit when you put some faces with the names. If you've managed to collect some photographs of your family and ancestors, make copies of them. You may have to cut them smaller to nestle them up in the branches, but it looks really cool when you're done. You can also glue on some photographs from the time when your ancestors were young. Find pictures of clothing or cars from back then and add them to your tree. It really brings history alive.

FUN FACT Leica, a world-renowned camera company, created a wall-mounted family tree showcasing its "family" of 107 cameras made from 1914 to 2014. The piece sold for $478,500 in 2016. *Smile!*

CASE FILES

FLOCKING TO U.S. CITIES

IN THE LATE 1800s, THE UNITED STATES BECAME A WORLDWIDE INDUSTRIAL POWER. THOUSANDS OF FACTORIES, MINES, AND WORKSHOPS SPREAD ACROSS THE COUNTRY, AND THEY NEEDED WORKERS. IMMIGRANTS ANSWERED THE CALL.

Between 1880 and 1920, nearly 24 million immigrants came to the U.S., with 1901 to 1910 being the single largest decade of immigration ever to that point. Most of the immigrants came from Europe, but it was a different mix than in earlier years. By 1900, migration had shifted east and south, with the new immigrants coming increasingly from Hungary, Italy, Poland, and Russia. Many were Catholic or Jewish, some Eastern Orthodox, and two-thirds settled in cities, forever transforming the United States. Families often immigrated together, though young men sometimes came first to find work and then sent for their families. In 1892, New York's Ellis Island opened to process immigrants, and smaller facilities opened at other port cities, including Angel Island near San Francisco.

To many native-born Americans, the influx of millions of new immigrants—often poor and speaking unfamiliar languages—was alarming. Some unfairly blamed the new arrivals for strikes and protests that resulted from the country's rapid industrialization, and they pressed the federal government to tighten immigration. Beginning with the Chinese Exclusion Act in 1882 and on through the 1920s, more laws restricted immigration and favored western Europeans, a preference that lasted until 1965.

RESEARCHING IMMIGRANTS OF THE 1880s TO 1920s

It's a thrill to connect your family heritage with the countries where your immigrant ancestors were born. Use your best genealogical detective skills to work back to those ancestors, and then look for the records that documented their arrival. Fortunately, there are lots of options. The federal censuses from 1850 to 1870 listed everyone's birthplace, and those from 1880 to 1930 included the parents' birthplaces, too. In addition, the federal government during this era required more documentation of immigration and naturalization than before. Federal immigration officials recorded immigrants starting in 1891, and many of those records are available online. Starting in 1906, naturalization records even gave the name of the ship, port, and date of arrival. New York's Ellis Island was the most common entry for immigrants in the late 19th and early 20th centuries, and you can search for your ancestor in a database of those arrivals. You may even find a picture of the ship they traveled on!

GET SMART FAST

INVESTIGATE	CLUES
Statue of Liberty–Ellis Island Foundation libertyellisfoundation.org	Searchable online database of immigrants arriving in New York from 1892 to 1957
National Archives Ethnic Heritage Links and Passenger Lists archives.gov/research/alic/reference/ethnic-heritage.html and aad.archives.gov/aad/series-list.jsp?cat=GP44	Links to many resources and records from around the world, records of passengers arriving from various countries
Immigration to the United States, 1789–1930 Harvard University Library ocp.hul.harvard.edu/immigration	Historical materials—books, pamphlets, serials, manuscripts, diaries, biographies, photographs, and more—documenting immigration to the United States
Cyndi's List cyndislist.com	Links to databases, how-to guides, and many resources for researching your heritage, including in other countries; look for a country under categories
Immigration History Research Center Archives, University of Minnesota lib.umn.edu/ihrca	Records of American ethnic communities originating in eastern, central, and southern Europe and the eastern Mediterranean
Genealogical societies tied to specific countries or ethnic groups	Search the Internet using the name of country or ethnic group, "historical" or "genealogical," and "society"
JewishGen jewishgen.org	Primary Internet source for Jewish genealogy includes thousands of databases, research tools, other resources
Ancestry.com	Contains ship passenger lists, citizenship and naturalization records, border crossing records, and more

FILLING IN THE BLANKS

So, you've identified your ancestors. You know where they were born and where they lived and died, but who were they *really*? What were their lives like? How did they get where they were, and what did they do between their B-day and D-day? It's time to find out. In this chapter, you'll dig deeper into their lives, finding the evidence to fill in those blanks and turn a family tree entry into a life's story.

FOLLOWING FOOTSTEPS

WHAT WAS IT LIKE FOR NONNO TONY, YOUR 4G-GRANDFATHER, TO TRAVEL TO AMERICA? Did he come alone or with his family? Was the ship he sailed on old and rickety or a luxurious ocean liner? Did he ever again get to see family members back in Sicily? Following an ancestor's journey across the ocean is one of the most rewarding parts of genealogical detective work—and, for a lot of genealogists, the goal of an investigation. Tracing your ancestors' footsteps can be challenging, but many resources provide the evidence you need to understand their immigration experience.

FUN FACT Most immigrants entered through five major ports: Philadelphia (the most popular port during the colonial era), New York, Boston, Baltimore, and New Orleans. By the mid-1800s, more immigrants arrived in New York than through all other ports combined.

GET CLUED IN

- **Motivation.** Deciding to move across the ocean, usually leaving family and friends behind, was not a decision made lightly. It took courage and optimism. Your ancestors often arrived with only what they could carry. They were risking everything, hoping that America offered the chance for a better life. What attracted them to America, and what drove them from their homes? Dig into the history of their original homelands to find out what motivated their migration.

- **Setting sail.** Most of our early immigrant ancestors arrived in ships, and documents related to these voyages provide some of the best evidence for tracing their journeys. Starting in 1820, the United States required ships to file passenger lists (or manifests) with customs officers in the port of arrival. The early lists included each passenger's name and any births or deaths that occurred during the voyage. Starting in 1883 in Philadelphia and in 1891 in other ports, immigration officials required even more information on immigration passenger lists, such as a passenger's occupation, marital status, health condition, and ability to read or write. The forms even recorded whether a passenger was coming to join a relative somewhere, who paid for the person's journey, and how much money the passenger was carrying!

- **Which ship?** If you can't find ship passenger lists, you can document your ancestor's voyage by finding immigration papers in America and emigration records from their country of origin. Remember that many U.S. census records included immigration information that can point you in the right direction. Some noted if a person had already become a citizen, or "naturalized." If it isn't obvious, look for the abbreviation "na" for naturalized or "al" for alien. (No, not the space kind: It means someone of foreign birth.)

GET SMART FAST

INVESTIGATE	CLUES
Passenger lists or manifests (also called customs passenger lists or manifests), 1820–1880s National Archives Digital copies online Ancestry.com FamilySearch.org and others	Each passenger's name, voyage information, births and deaths on voyage
Immigration passenger lists or manifests, after late 1880s National Archives Digital copies online Ancestry.com FamilySearch.org and others	Each passenger's name, place of birth, last residence, age, occupation, and gender; ship's name, ports of departure and arrival, and date of arrival
Library of Congress loc.gov/search/?q=Immigration loc.gov/rr/genealogy/bib_guid/immigrant	Numerous materials related to immigration, including general works in immigration, passenger lists, ship information, immigrant experience, personal narratives, and correspondence
Spartacus Educational spartacus-educational.com/USAimmigration.htm	European immigration, including information about the journey, background on countries of origin, and biographies of interesting immigrants

INCREASE YOUR CULTURAL IQ

WHO ARE YOU? NO, NOT JUST YOUR NAME. There's more to you than that, right? Think about it. There are lots of ways you can identify yourself: star soccer player, brilliant student, mischievous prankster, American or Filipino or Bengali or French or ... what else? The same was true for your ancestors. They had multiple identities. If they were recent immigrants, they may have identified strongly with two places: America, and their homeland. Interesting trivia? Oh, it's far more than that! It's a clue.

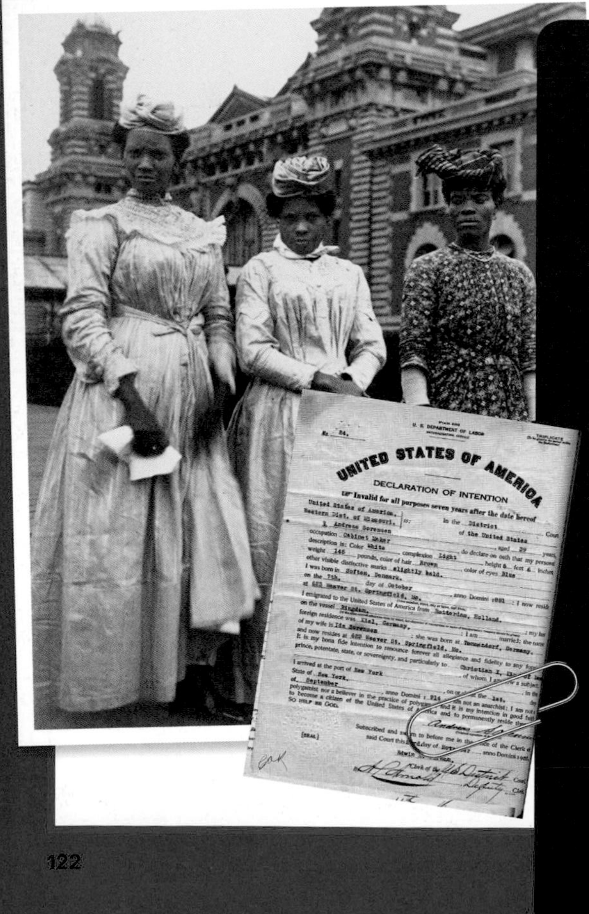

BECOMING AMERICAN

At some point, your immigrant ancestors may have decided to be "naturalized," that is, to become citizens of their new country. The naturalization process has changed throughout the centuries of our country's existence: different requirements, different forms, different everything. But, generally, four steps stayed the same from 1795 through the early 1930s. Your ancestors filled out a Declaration of Intention ("first papers"), renouncing citizenship in their previous country and any allegiance to that country and its ruler. No more bowing before the king! The "intent" part meant your ancestors intended to become U.S. citizens. (After 1824, millions of immigrants who arrived as kids could skip this step.) The next step, the Petition for Naturalization ("final papers"), certified that your ancestors met all the requirements for citizenship, including living in the United States for a certain period of time, and were formally requesting to become citizens. At the time citizenship was granted, your ancestors probably signed an Oath of Allegiance to the United States and were issued a Certificate of Naturalization, the formal document of citizenship. Whew! Lots of documents—but that means lots of clues!

GET CLUED IN

- **Traditions.** You can learn a lot about your ancestors' lives by exploring your family customs: that special food you have on New Year's, family recipes your aunt always prepares, lullabies your grandmother sang to you in another language. Find out the stories behind them. Even if you don't know for sure where your ancestors came from, a family custom can be the clue you need.

- **World travelers.** Immigration may not have been the only time your ancestors journeyed overseas. Check to see if they had passports, the official government document that certified their identity and citizenship so they could travel abroad. To get passports, they had to fill out an application with lots of personal information and probably even where they intended to travel. Maybe they were returning to their homeland for a visit.

- **Photographic evidence.** It's great when you have old family photos—even if you have no idea who those people were! Study their clothes, hairstyles, and jewelry for clues about their lives. If you're not sure where your ancestors lived, these old photos may provide additional clues. If they are mounted on card stock, look for the photographer's name and location. You may be able to place your relatives by researching where the photo studio was located. There weren't that many places to have a photographic portrait made back in the late 1800s and early 1900s.

GET SMART FAST

INVESTIGATE	CLUES
Naturalization information National Archives archives.gov/research/naturalization	Details on naturalization records and where to find them
Naturalization documents Digital copies online at Fold3.com, FamilySearch.org, and others	Detailed information about a person, including name, country of origin, physical description, and more
Countries and their Cultures: Multicultural America everyculture.com/multi	Articles with overview of countries, information about immigration to the United States, settlement patterns, cultural traditions, and more

DID YOU KNOW?

As millions of immigrants came to America in the late 1800s and early 1900s, various "Americanization" programs helped them adjust to their new way of life. Community centers offered free classes on citizenship requirements, factories provided English lessons after work hours, and towns held festive Americanization Days to help instill national pride. And, yes, kids got the days off school.

PUT TOGETHER A FAMILY COOKBOOK

Maybe it's the smell of a freshly baked apple strudel, the crunch of a toasty potato latke, or the melt-in-your-mouth warmth of a homemade enchilada, but nothing says "family" like a favorite family recipe. Maybe your family has recipes that have been handed down from generation to generation. These foods—and the stories that go along with them—are part of your heritage. Understanding the foods your ancestors liked to cook and eat will help you understand more about them—and about you. Collect the special recipes in a family cookbook. It's a fun and tasty way to celebrate your family's history.

1. DECISIONS

Before you gather the recipes, decide how you want the book to look and how you're going to keep the recipes together. Are you going to put them into a loose-leaf binder, staple pages of them together, or have the local copy shop spiral-bind them?

2. GATHER

Tell family members about your project and ask them to send you a favorite family recipe, one that they fondly remember from growing up. Ask them to double-check the recipe by making it, so you're sure no ingredients are left out. Find out if anyone has recipes written out by ancestors and try to get good-quality copies of those to include. This is a great time to reach out to those distant cousins!

3. STORIES

Ask your family members why the recipes are special. Did they eat the food on holidays or other occasions? Ask them to share stories or traditions associated with the food.

4. PHOTOS

Gather photographs of family members and ancestors who made the special foods or passed down the recipes. Don't forget photos of current family members who like to serve these recipes.

5. ORGANIZE

Decide what order you want to put the recipes in. Do you want to group them by categories, such as main courses, desserts, or appetizers? Or perhaps you want to organize them by holiday, branch of the family, or generation?

6. ASSEMBLE

Put your family cookbook together. Even if you decide to type up all the recipes so they're easy to read, include copies of the recipes written out by ancestors. It's cool to see the recipes in their handwriting. Include the stories and traditions associated with the food, and add photos of past and current family members who make the dishes. (Tip: It's best to scan the photos and handwritten recipes and then add copies of them to the page.)

7. TASTE

Prepare the recipes and enjoy them!

8. SHARE

Make copies of the family cookbook to share with other family members. They make great gifts!

A GOOD START

Special foods eaten on New Year's can bring you luck throughout the year! At least, that's the belief in cultures around the world. For many Italians, lentils and slices of sausage bring good fortune, because they (loosely) resemble coins. Pork and cabbage, often pickled to become sauerkraut, are the centerpiece of New Year's meals for many people with central European heritage, such as Germans, Hungarians, Czechs, and Poles. Shiny, silver-scaled herring, often pickled, is a must-have New Year's dish for many Scandinavian, Nordic, Polish, Baltic, and Jewish communities. In the American South, there's an old saying: "Peas for pennies, greens for dollars, and cornbread for gold." For many families, especially in the African-American community, this means the New Year must start with Hoppin' John, a dish made with black-eyed peas and rice. Black-eyed peas, with their promise to grow when planted, symbolize good things to come.

LAND HO!

WITH ALL THE LAND OUT THERE, YOU'D THINK GENEALOGISTS WOULD FLOCK TO LAND RECORDS FOR INFORMATION. But, no. Land and property records are among the least-used resources—probably because they're the most poorly understood. And that's a shame, because besides rooting your ancestors to a physical space, they often provide other pieces of evidence valuable to genealogical detectives. Here's what you need to know to get started with them.

EXPERT TIP

THE **FEDERAL GOVERNMENT** DISTRIBUTED LAND IN 30 STATES. THESE "PUBLIC DOMAIN" LANDS WERE **DIVIDED** ALONG A GRID INTO **TRACTS, TOWNSHIPS, SECTIONS, AND PARCELS.** PROPERTY IN THE ORIGINAL COLONIES AND NEIGHBORING STATES WAS DIVIDED BY **LANDSCAPE FEATURES** AND **CONTROLLED** BY STATES. LOOK FOR "STATE LAND" RECORDS IN STATE ARCHIVES.

DID YOU KNOW?

During the American Revolution, there was no federal government. That made it hard to pay soldiers who fought for the country's independence. Some were paid with land, known as "bounty land." Women who provided aid or supplies to the military received land, too. Bounty lands were also given out after the War of 1812, early Indian Wars, and Mexican War.

GET CLUED IN

- **Federal.** The records we're talking about here cover the transfer of property from the United States government to an individual or family, not the sale of property from one family to another. These federal records provide details about when and where your ancestors obtained that land—and maybe additional clues about their family.

- **Land grab.** After the American Revolution, the federal government figured out ways to divide and distribute land. Some was sold to raise money and pay off war debts, and some eventually was used to entice westward migration and settlement. The Homestead Act of 1862 allowed citizens to each claim 160 acres (65 hectares) in federal land, as long as they lived on it and farmed it for five years. Women could homestead, too, and these records are a great find.

- **Who's nearby?** After finding what piece of property you ancestor got from the government, look at neighboring properties. Neighbors sometimes turn out to be relatives!

Poster circa 1880 advertising the opportunity for settlers "to secure Free Land and Homes"

GET SMART FAST

INVESTIGATE	CLUES
Guide to United States Bureau of Land Management Tract Books FamilySearch.org familysearch.org/wiki/en/United_States,_Bureau_of_Land_Management_Tract_Books_(FamilySearch_Historical_Records)	Resources and tips for searching for land records; background on available records in 30 states (generally west of the original 13 Colonies and their immediate neighbors)
Homestead Records Bureau of Land Management, U.S. Department of the Interior glorecords.blm.gov	Searchable index of eight million land titles given to individuals, 1820–1908, with description of land. Note: Only people who actually were granted a federal land patent are included; two million case files were never completed and aren't listed.
Federal "bounty land" records Digitized and indexed online Ancestry.com FamilySearch.org Fold3.com	Land records, applications with information about person's military service or support to military (including by women)
State land records familysearch.org/wiki/en/State_Land	Guide to finding land records for the 20 "state land" states: the original 13 Colonies, states created from them, plus Texas and Hawaii

UNCLE SAM WANTS YOU!

MILITARY SERVICE IS ONE OF THE MOST DOCUMENTED TIMES IN SOMEONE'S LIFE. Even before people make it to boot camp, they've made a paper trail, and it continues long after they leave the service. Learning about your ancestors' military service can add historical context to their lives. It also can provide a wealth of detailed information about them and their families that has little to do with the military. Even if you don't know if an ancestor served in the military, it's worth checking.

EXPERT TIP

EVEN IF YOUR **ANCESTOR DIDN'T SERVE**, HE MAY HAVE HAD TO REGISTER FOR THE **DRAFT** OR **SELECTIVE SERVICE**. FINDING A DRAFT CARD CAN NOT ONLY HELP YOU LEARN ABOUT POSSIBLE **MILITARY SERVICE** BUT ALSO PROVIDE OTHER DATA ABOUT YOUR ANCESTOR.

GET CLUED IN

- **Helpful start.** It can aid your search for records if you can first find out when and where your ancestor served, what branch of the military your ancestor was in, and whether he or she was in the enlisted ranks or an officer.

- **Not sure?** Veterans sometimes don't want to talk about their experiences, so you don't always know if an ancestor served. It's worth searching just in case, especially if you have a male ancestor who was between 18 and 30 years old during a time of war (or younger for early wars). Here's another clue: If your ancestor got married at an older age than was typical back then, it may have been because he was in the military earlier. Sometimes grave markers refer to military service.

- **Records.** You may find "compiled service records," which include information from muster rolls ("muster" means to assemble troops for battle, inspection, or exercises), pay vouchers, and other records that will tell you your ancestor's service as well as other information.

- **Afterward.** Pension records—both applications and recorded payments—for veterans, their widows, and other heirs may be even more interesting to a genealogical detective, because they often contain supporting documents, such as narratives of events during service, marriage certificates, birth records, death certificates, letters, and even pages from family Bibles.

GET SMART FAST

INVESTIGATE	CLUES
Veterans History Project Library of Congress loc.gov/vets/	Personal accounts of American war veterans and civilians who supported their efforts, from World War I onward
Civil War Soldiers and Sailors Database National Park Service nps.gov/civilwar/soldiers-and-sailors-database.htm	Index of men who served in the Civil War, both Union and Confederate, with basic information, such as name, rank, and unit
Online military records and indexes FamilySearch.org Ancestry.com Fold3.com	Indexes and some full service records, with information about rank, unit, where person served; basic biographical information; medical information; and more
United States Military Online Genealogy Records familysearch.org/wiki/en/United_States_Military_Online_Genealogy_Records	Links to U.S. military databases and collections, including indexes and digital images, for service, pension, draft registration, roster lists, and more
National Archives Washington, D.C. archives.gov/veterans	Guidance in researching and requesting military service records
National Personnel Records Center National Archives St. Louis, Missouri archives.gov/st-louis/military-personnel	Military records of discharged and deceased veterans of all services during the 20th century
Online Military Indexes and Records Maintained by Joe Beine militaryindexes.com	Links to websites with records related to Revolutionary War, War of 1812, Mexican-American War, Civil War, Spanish-American War, World Wars I and II, Korean War, and Vietnam War

DIGGING INTO DAILY LIFE

HOW DO WE SPEND OUR DAYS? Most of the time we're not moving to a different country, marching with the military, or taking up property. Instead, we're going to school or work, maybe playing sports or games, or attending religious services or get-togethers. The same was true of your ancestors. If you really want to understand them, dig into their daily lives.

GET CLUED IN

- **School spirit.** The school years—up through college for a lot of people—are some of the most important in your ancestors' lives. Many schools and colleges have directories or yearbooks of students. Not only may you find a picture of Great-grandpa Leland, but you may learn about activities and clubs he joined.

- **Heigh-ho, heigh-ho ...** If you didn't find them digging through the drawers in your parents' home, it may be tough to find employment records for your ancestors. Employers may not release these records, but you may find old employee newsletters and reports that give you insight into your ancestors' work experience.

- **Social Security.** These days, Americans get a Social Security number when they're children, often at birth. It wasn't always that way. Most people waited until they entered the workforce, and they often listed their employer on their application—along with lots of personal data. If you can find your ancestor's Social Security number, you can request your ancestor's application from the Social Security Administration for a fee.

- **Where there's a will ...** Many people create a will, which expresses their final wishes about what should happen to their property and belongings after they die, who should care for their pets or children (if any are minors), and more. A will, often filed at a county courthouse, can give a fascinating glimpse into your ancestor's thoughts and priorities.

DID YOU KNOW?

For centuries, Hindu family histories have been kept on long scrolls at holy sites throughout India, many at the ancient city of Haridwar. A Brahmin pandit (priest), popularly known as a "panda," keeps the handwritten scrolls for a specific region, passing them down from generation to generation. Hindus still can find their family's panda and record events on their scroll.

GET SMART FAST

INVESTIGATE	CLUES
College and school yearbooks, organization and religious institution histories and records Search online for the institution's name and "yearbook" or "history."	Photos of your ancestors, their activities, and clubs and religious institutions or organizations they joined
Employee Records From *The Source*, 3rd ed., edited by L. Szucs and Luebking (2006) at ancestry.com/wiki/index.php?title=Employee_Records	Guide to locating all types of employee records, including those related to apprenticeships, labor unions, railroad employees, government personnel, and Social Security
Social Security Death Index Online FamilySearch.org Ancestry.com	For people who died after 1962: Social Security number, name, date of birth and death, residence at time of application, location where death benefits paid
Probate Records familysearch.org/wiki/en/United_States_Probate_Records	Guide to probate records, what they contain, where to find them; FamilySearch also has some records online.

TIME TRAVEL

THERE'S NO BETTER WAY TO GET A FEEL FOR AN ANCESTOR'S LIFE THAN TO EXPERIENCE IT YOURSELF. No, we're not actually talking about time travel. But that would be so awesome! You can experience past eras vicariously, through the eyes of another person. The best way to do that is to dive into history. There are lots of ways to do it, and some of them do require travel! Get ready to experience what life was like for your ancestors.

DID YOU KNOW?

In West Africa, a griot (historian, storyteller, musician, and poet) keeps an oral history of a society. Traditionally, a person had to be born into a griot family, but schools now teach these arts. Today, griots travel all over singing and playing traditional instruments and presiding at ceremonies—and, of course, remembering a society's important moments.

GET CLUED IN

- **Live it.** If you can't time travel back to your ancestor's era, visiting a living history museum is the next best thing. These museums often include replicas of settlements, buildings, or ships. Costumed interpreters bring the places to life by reenacting town life, farming, or even battles. You can also tour old mines or places your ancestors may have passed through, like Ellis Island.

- **A good book.** Curl up with the story of some place your ancestors lived. Histories written about a limited area, such as a town or county, can tell you what life was like when your ancestors were there. Look in nearby libraries and historical societies. If you can't get there, check out the American Folklife Center's collection at the Library of Congress; much of it is digitized and available online.

- **The spoken word.** Maybe your great-grandfather didn't leave an oral history, but many others did. Find the story of someone who came to America from your great-grandfather's country at roughly the same time, and you'll have a good feel for his life on both sides of the ocean.

- **Worldview.** We've said it before, but it's worth repeating: To understand why your ancestors left their original homeland to come to America, read about what was happening in their homeland and over here. It may help you appreciate why your ancestors made the move.

AWESOME LIVING HISTORY MUSEUMS

We could fill an entire book with amazing living history museums and experiences. Here are some great ones to check out:

Bodie State Historic Park
Bridgeport, California
www.parks.ca.gov/bodie

Civil War Battle Reenactment
Gettysburg National Military Park
Gettysburg, Pennsylvania
gettysburgreenactment.com

Colonial Williamsburg
Williamsburg, Virginia
colonialwilliamsburg.com

Conner Prairie Interactive History Park
Fishers, Indiana, near Indianapolis
connerprairie.org

Greenfield Village
Dearborn, Michigan
thehenryford.org/visit/greenfield-village

Lincoln Log Cabin State Historic Site
Lerna, Illinois
lincolnlogcabin.org

LSU Rural Life Museum
Baton Rouge, Louisiana
lsu.edu/rurallife

Old Cowtown
Wichita, Kansas
oldcowtown.org

Old Sturbridge Village
Sturbridge, Massachusetts
osv.org

Old World Wisconsin
Eagle, Wisconsin
oldworldwisconsin.wisconsinhistory.org

Plimoth Plantation
Plymouth, Massachusetts, between Boston and Cape Cod
plimoth.org

Stuhr Museum of the Prairie Pioneer
Grand Island, Nebraska
stuhrmuseum.org

Vermilionville Historic Village
Lafayette, Louisiana
vermilionville.org

TRACE YOUR FAMILY'S JOURNEY

You've followed your ancestors' journeys from place to place, maybe even across the ocean, or from sea to shining sea. It took a lot of work to track them, and it's an amazing accomplishment—one you should show off! A great way to display your family's journey is to plot it on a map. Here are some tips for making a display-worthy piece of family art.

1. LOCAL OR GLOBAL

Decide if you want to focus on your family's journey for all the generations you documented, or if you'd like to zoom in on more recent generations. If you trace all generations, you may want to show their journeys on a world map. If you want to focus on a more recent time period, you can probably get by with a map of the United States.

2. PREPARE THE MAP

Get a nice-quality map and have it mounted on foam board at a frame shop. (If you want to try to mount it yourself, you'll need an adult to help you. Instructions can be found on the Internet.) Consider whether you want a frame for it, too. Yes, you also can map a journey online, if you wish. If that seems fun, go for it. (A good, free option is *scribblemaps.com,* but be sure to get a parent's permission to go online.) And remember that it's a little harder to display that on your wall!

3. PREPARE YOURSELF

Gather a list of all the places your ancestors lived. Decide if you also want to include milestones in their lives, such as where they got married and where their children were born—maybe even where they worked or went to school (if your map is detailed enough). List the places by the date a family was there.

EXPERT TIP

REMEMBER THAT COUNTRY AND COUNTY BORDERS HAVE CHANGED OVER THE YEARS. YOU MAY HAVE TO DO A LITTLE DETECTIVE WORK TO FIGURE OUT EXACTLY WHERE TO PLOT YOUR ANCESTORS' EARLY HOMES AND JOURNEYS. FIND MAPS FROM WHEN YOUR ANCESTORS LIVED IN THOSE PLACES. CHECK OUT CHAPTER 1, PAGE 27, FOR SOME GREAT RESOURCES.

4. ASSIGN COLORS

Pick different colors for different family lines, and maybe even for different generations. Remember those colors you used to organize your files? They may be good options. Or just pick some that look good with the map.

5. PLOT

Plot your ancestors' paths on the map, one family at a time, from as far back as you can right up to today. There are several ways to do this. You can use permanent markers to draw on the map. Or, if you want to have a little more artsy fun, string different color yarn from place to place and use push pins to hold it in place. Mark locations of milestones either with pens or additional push pins. You'll find that all the paths converge on you!

6. LABEL

If you wish, you can label the milestones with dates or other information.

7. HANG IT UP

Find a place to display your family's journey.

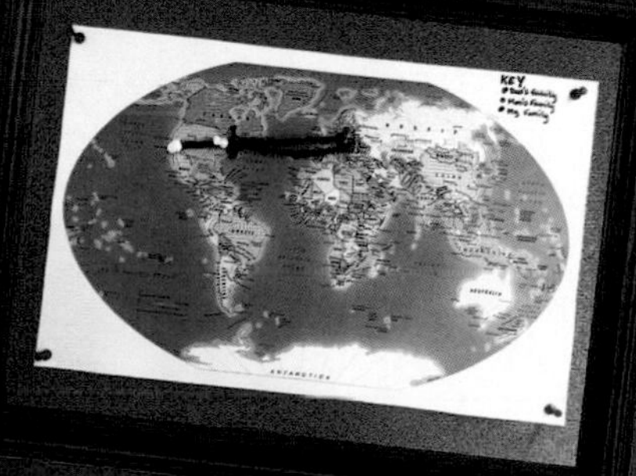

DID YOU KNOW?

A map is flat, right? Earth, of course, is not. That creates a challenge for mapmakers! Imagine cutting a globe in half and smooshing it down flat. Some parts would wrinkle up and others would tear apart. The size, shape, and location of different features would change. Mapmakers must decide where to allow distortion and where not to.

RESEARCH ROADBLOCK VANISHED WITHOUT A TRACE?

YOUR ANCESTOR WAS A GREAT MAGICIAN. He must have been. One moment he was there, the next he was gone. *Abracadabra!* Vanished without a trace. Harry Houdini himself couldn't pull off a better disappearing act. Or, maybe your ancestor did the opposite trick: He magically appeared in town, complete with a loving spouse, adorable children, and cute pets out of nowhere.

How did they do it? It's probably safe to rule out magic tricks, alien abductions, or the witness protection program. When an ancestor disappears or appears out of nowhere, it can be a genealogical detective's worst nightmare—but that's about it. It's a cold trail, not an indication of early invisibility cloaks or extraterrestrial interactions. *(But if it were, that'd be really cool to document.)*

Is this the end of your investigation? Will your family tree never branch out? Sometimes,

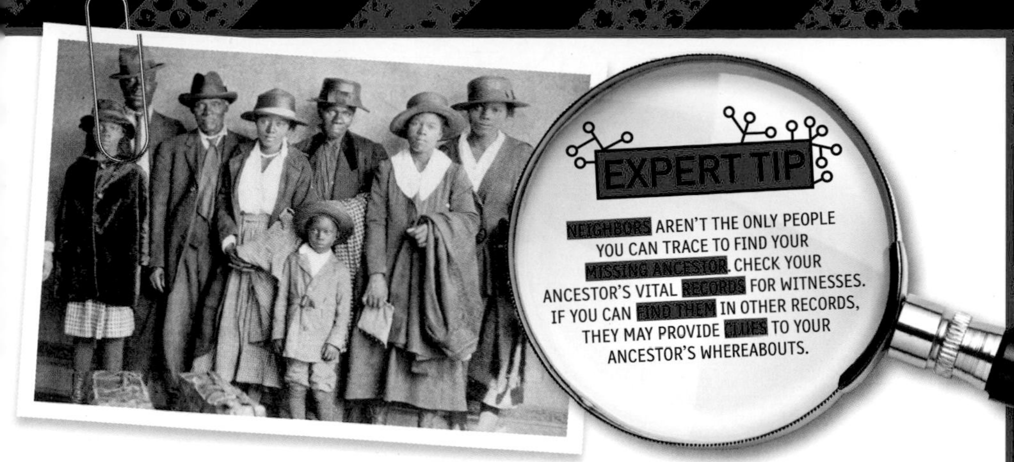

yes. (Sorry.) But don't give up yet. You often can solve the case of the missing relative or unknown past with some extra resourceful detective work.

Get neighborly. In both cases, the first place to look is at the neighbors. No, not because they're suspects. They actually can help you out. For a disappearing act, go back to the census records where you last saw your ancestor. Find four or so neighbors on either side of your ancestor. Then move forward to the next census and find the neighbors. When you locate the census page, search up and down it for your ancestor. If one or more of the neighbors is gone, too, it means you need to widen your search. Families often moved with relatives and friends, so search for your ancestor and the missing neighbor. Start looking in neighboring counties. If you can dig up some information on migration patterns at the time (check county histories), use that to guide your search. If you know your ancestor's religion, look for the next county with the same kind of church or other religious institution.

If your ancestor appeared out of nowhere, use the same technique in reverse. Find your ancestor's neighbors in the census, and then search for the neighbors in earlier censuses. Be sure to look at the actual records (digitized is fine) and review many entries on both sides. (The census taker didn't always go in order.) Other places to check in both cases are property records, voter registration records, the U.S. census mortality schedules of 1850 through 1880, and state censuses of 1885. This is the time to pull out all the stops. Search all available records—online and in libraries, historical societies, and archives. When you finally find what happened to your ancestor, it'll feel like you pulled off the most awesome magic trick yourself!

CASE FILES

THE GREAT MIGRATION

THE LARGEST INTERNAL MIGRATION IN U.S. HISTORY OCCURRED IN THE EARLY 20TH CENTURY. During World War I, as immigration from Europe slowed, thousands of African Americans left the South and moved to northern cities. By 1930, as many as two million African Americans had made the Great Migration. At first, most moved to New York, Chicago, Detroit, and Pittsburgh. By the 1940s, they had gone as far as the West Coast, settling in San Francisco, Los Angeles, and Oakland, California; Seattle, Washington; and Portland, Oregon.

Like the Europeans who had arrived earlier, African Americans left the South in search of better lives. The major black newspaper, the *Chicago Defender*, ran news stories about the job opportunities in the North, and northern factories recruited African-American workers. At the time, many African Americans in the South were renting land to farm at terms that made it nearly impossible to make a living. So when the boll weevil (an invasive species of beetle that eats cotton buds) ruined their crops, they had little reason to stay.

Economic opportunities in the North were not the only reason for the Great Migration. Beginning about a dozen years after the end of the Civil War, laws enforcing racial segregation (called Jim Crow laws) greatly limited social, educational, economic, and political opportunities for African Americans. Many moved north because they refused to tolerate these unjust social practices any longer.

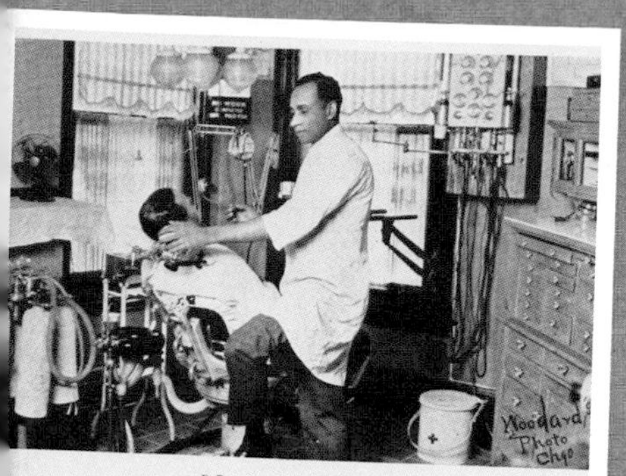

DR. C. JESSE DAVIS

Dr. C. Jesse Davis, graduate of Meharry Medical College, Nashville, Tenn., in his dental suite in the Roosevelt Bank Building at 35th Street and Grand Boulevard. Dr. Davis is one of the 85 colored Dentists who are contributing, through application of the most approved dental methods, to the preservation of the health of the masses in Chicago.

RESEARCHING THE GREAT MIGRATION

To trace your ancestors back to the Old South, you need to find their names and addresses and, of course, make sure you have the right people! First find them in the 1940 census, when they probably were living in northern cities. The 1940 census will tell you the state where they were born and also their address in 1935. Compare the 1935 residence and the place of birth to see if your ancestors were already settled or still on the move. Find vital records of all the family members to discover where and when children were born—another helpful clue. Use earlier census records and city directories to trace ancestors as they migrated northward. Other records also provide helpful information. Check military records. Men had to register for the draft in World War I and World War II, and some may even have served in the Union Army during the Civil War. Finally, look through newspapers. Not only can they give you a great idea of what life was like, but they may even mention your family members.

GET SMART FAST

INVESTIGATE	CLUES
Census records FamilySearch.org Ancestry.com (Ancestry.com can be searched free of charge through many libraries)	Address, age, birthplace, race; in 1910, Civil War veteran (marked "UA" for Union veteran, including U.S. "Colored" Troops)
City directories Libraries in hometowns Some online at FamilySearch.org and Ancestry.com and other sites	Names (wife's sometimes listed after husband's), addresses, occupations, possibly death dates, forwarding addresses for people who have moved
Military records FamilySearch.org Ancestry.com Fold3.com	Indexes and some full-service records, including basic biographical information, address, and more
Newspapers chroniclingamerica.loc.gov	Accounts of life; "Colored Society" sections that note births, visits, anniversaries, etc.
"Born in Slavery: Slave Narratives from the Federal Writers' Project, 1936 to 1938" loc.gov/collections/slave-narratives-from-the-federal-writers-project-1936-to-1938	More than 2,300 first-person accounts of slavery and 500 photographs of former slaves

EXPERT TIP

SOME CITY DIRECTORIES LONG AGO IDENTIFIED AFRICAN AMERICANS BY RACE. IT'S AN OFFENSIVE IDEA, BUT IT CAN HELP YOU IDENTIFY YOUR ANCESTORS. LOOK FOR (C) OR (COL.) FOR "COLORED," (NEG.) FOR "NEGRO," OR A * SYMBOL AFTER A PERSON'S NAME. SOME DIRECTORIES ALSO HAD SEPARATE SECTIONS FOR AFRICAN AMERICANS.

INTO THE FORENSICS LAB

You're a terrific genealogical detective, but try as you might, you won't find documents linking your family back to your most ancient ancestors. That type of evidence didn't exist back then! So if you want to find your earliest origins—or cousins you never knew you had—genetic genealogy may provide the answers. In the next pages, you'll learn about what some laboratory tests can tell you—and what they can't.

1 1 0 0 1 0 1 1 0 1 0 0 1 0 1
0 1 0 0 1 0 1 0 1 1 0 1 0 1 1
0 0 1 0 1 1 0 1 0 0 1 0 0 1 1
0 1 0 1 1 0 0 1 1 1 0 1 0 0 1
0 0 1 1 0 1 0 1 1 0 0 0 1 0 1
N
N
H
AGCATGGAC
ACATTACCA
AGCTAGTTA
GCTTAGTCA
ATGCATTAC
GTAGGACT
GCAATTCAT
GCAATTGCG
GGACTGCA
ATTCATGCA
ATTGCGAGC
ATGGACACA
TAGTTAGCT
TAGTCAATG

YOUR BLUEPRINT

HAS ANYONE EVER SAID YOU HAVE YOUR GRANDDAD'S EYES OR YOUR MOM'S MUSICAL ABILITY? How'd you get them? A lot of what makes you *you* is your heredity, the genetic information passed from your biological parents to you. Your genetic makeup influences all sorts of traits—how you look, your personality, even your ability to play guitar or hit a softball. Of course, your genetic makeup doesn't determine everything. All sorts of things influence who you become: How your parents raise you, where you live, how you take care of your body, what interests you pursue, school, friends, and on and on. Still, our genetic code holds so much fascinating information, scientists like to study it. It can even tie you to ancestors *waaaay* back in time.

HAPLO-*WHAT?*

GET CLUED IN

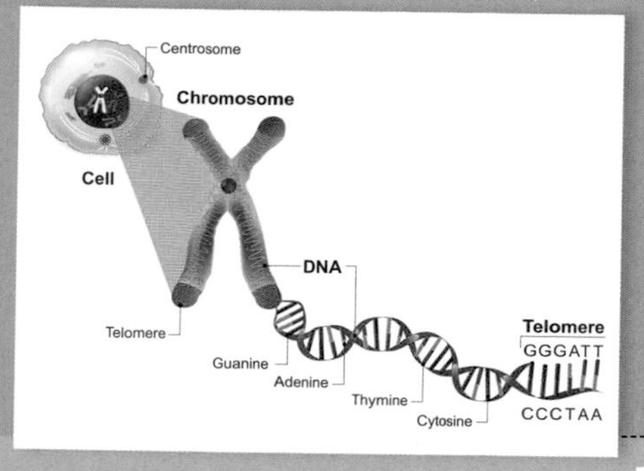

- **DNA.** Every one of us has a unique chemical blueprint that affects who we are. That chemical is ... ready for this? ... deoxyribonucleic acid. Just call it DNA. It's an amazing chemical in every one of your cells, and it holds the instructions for your body's growth and all sorts of traits, including whether you're a boy or a girl, tall or short, and so on. It's shaped like a long spiral staircase. (But much, much smaller.)

- **Genes.** DNA carries special codes, called genes, for making every part of you. Each gene is like a recipe—except it's not written with words; it's written with four DNA chemicals in different patterns. Some are recipes for making your characteristics, such as your brown eyes and straight, black hair. Others are recipes for how your body works. Each of us has about 20,000 different genes.

- **Chromosomes.** Genes are packaged into structures called chromosomes, tiny spaghetti-like structures inside of cells. We have 23 pairs of chromosomes in each cell. Why do we say pairs? Each of your biological parents gives you 23 chromosomes. The chromosomes come in different lengths and patterns. The first 22 of them are called autosomes. The final pair, the sex chromosomes, determine whether you're a boy or a girl.

DID YOU KNOW?

Identical twins aren't completely identical. They have the same DNA, so they look alike (and can pull all sorts of awesome identity-swapping tricks on their parents). But their fingerprints aren't the same. The ridges, swirls, and valleys of our fingerprints get changed a bit before we're born. Twins' positions inside their mother's womb—what they're pushing against and where their hands develop—subtly change their fingerprints. Kinda limits what they can get away with, doesn't it?

DECODING YOUR DNA

HOW'D YOU LIKE TO FIND A BUNCH OF RELATIVES—BOTH CLOSE COUSINS AND DISTANT RELATIVES—IN ONE EASY STEP? That may be possible with genetic genealogy, an approach that uses a simple DNA test to help you find your kin. For genealogical detectives who can't uncover enough evidence to link generations into the past, genetic genealogy can speed them past roadblocks. If you want to go way back into your past to find your deep ancestral heritage, genetic genealogy also will help identify the haplogroup you belong to. But genetic genealogy tests can't tell you everything, so make sure you know what you're getting and if it's what you want to know. None of the tests are free.

NO STUDYING REQUIRED!

Are you ready to take a science test that covers thousands of years of genetic heredity? Gulp. Sounds hard, doesn't it? But it's not. It's as easy as spitting. Seriously. For some of the tests, all you need to do is provide a saliva sample. For others, you simply swab the inside of your cheek.

GET CLUED IN

- **Deep ancestry.** Genetic genealogy finds your haplogroup by comparing your DNA to genetic mutations dating from thousands of years ago. Haplogroups are genetic populations associated with certain regions. So you might learn that you have ancestors from South Asia or Europe or the Middle East. But don't expect the test to tell you if your family's background is Irish or French. In some cases, mutations are specific enough that tests can link you to more precise areas or even surnames, but most of the time, they won't be that exact.

- **Results vary.** Scientists have to interpret the results based on other DNA samples they have, which vary from one testing company to another. If you test with more than one company, you may get different results. But as the companies get larger pools of DNA for comparison, the results will become more consistent.

- **Cousins.** Many of the tests let you connect with others with similar stands of DNA, so you can find relatives you may not have known about earlier—as long as they also tested themselves and made their results available.

- **Testing what?** Not all tests use the same genetic material or look for the same kind of results. The most popular tests combine autosomal DNA and admixture analysis. An autosomal DNA test (atDNA), which looks at all ancestral lines, is most accurate up to the second-cousin level, while an admixture analysis seeks a person's geographical origins based on an analysis of his or her genetic ancestry. Of the other tests, a Y-DNA test, only for males, looks only at the paternal line and can be used to connect male relatives, but it does not show how many generations back they're related. A mitochondrial DNA (mtDNA) test, available for both females and males, traces a person's maternal line.

GET SMART FAST

INVESTIGATE	CLUES
Family Tree DNA familytreedna.com	Genealogical, personal ancestry (autosomal) test
Ancestry.com's DNA test dna.ancestry.com	Genealogical, personal ancestry (autosomal) test
23andMe 23andme.com	Genealogical, personal ancestry, medical (but limited by U.S. government) test
National Geographic Society Genographic Project Geno 2.0 Next Generation genographic.national geographic.com	Population genetics research, personal ancestry (autosomal), personal ancestry (Y-DNA), personal ancestry (mtDNA) test
International Society of Genetic Genealogy isogg.org/wiki/Autosomal_DNA_testing_comparison_chart	Information about genetic genealogy, including table comparing various DNA tests

EXPERT TIP

DON'T RELY ON ANY ONE SOURCE FOR YOUR GENEALOGICAL INVESTIGATION. DNA TESTS CAN PROVIDE GREAT BACKGROUND, BUT THEY CAN'T TELL YOU EVERYTHING ABOUT YOUR FAMILY HISTORY. (SOME PEOPLE WHO'VE TRIED MULTIPLE DNA TESTS HAVE GOTTEN QUITE DIFFERENT RESULTS FROM EACH ONE.) BUT SOMETIMES A DNA TEST CAN SUPPLY THE MISSING PIECE FOR YOUR GENEALOGICAL PUZZLE.

MAKE YOUR CASE

***WHEW!* YOU HAVE DONE SO MUCH WORK INVESTIGATING YOUR FAMILY BACKGROUND.** Well done, Detective, well done! But before you breathe a sigh of relief, kick your feet up, and watch a movie, you've got a little more work to do. You've built an airtight case for your heritage. The last thing you want is to lose it. Fortunately, you have lots of options for preserving the evidence.

SHARE YOUR FINDINGS

More than ever before, you realize you have a big, interesting family out there. Chances are, most of your relatives would love to know more about your clan, too. You can share your family tree and heritage in many ways. Many of the online genealogy sites let you give family members access to your family tree, but that's not the only way to share your family heritage. Scan old family photographs and load them onto picture-sharing sites, or create a private family website using a host that has special settings for closed groups. (Be sure to get your parents' permission before you do anything online.) Don't be limited to sharing evidence you've uncovered. Be creative and pull your work together into an awesome presentation. You could use a program like PowerPoint or Google Slides to bring in photographs and stories in addition to your family tree. It'd be the highlight of a family reunion or other gathering. Consider making a book with family stories, interesting facts, and your family tree. Some genealogists get so inspired by the stories they unearth that they write entire family histories.

GET CLUED IN

- **Online.** Several genealogical websites let you build your family tree online and save supporting documentation that you've found on their sites to your family tree. But what if it's a fee-based site, and you don't plan to renew your subscription? You don't want it stuck there, right? What many people don't realize is that it's possible to download all that information onto your own computer, as long as you have an app or software that can handle the files.

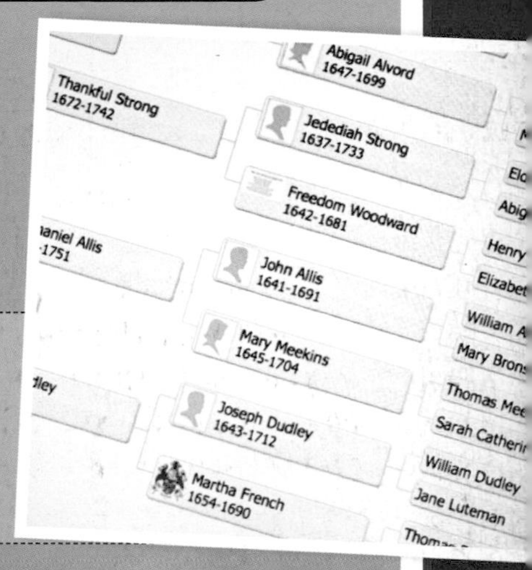

- **On your device.** You can get computer software or tablet apps that let you keep your family tree on your own device. Because technology changes so quickly, make sure the files are kept in formats that can be transferred to other programs or devices when you need to upgrade.

- **Tame the papers.** Make sure all your evidence is properly filed away, with original documents, photographs, and artifacts preserved in archival-quality materials. Remember all that work you did to set up an organized system for keeping track of your evidence? (What?! You don't? Take a look back at chapter 2.) Be sure you use that system!

DID YOU KNOW?

Boy Scouts can earn a merit badge for genealogy. You have to demonstrate your genealogical knowledge by meeting nine requirements. But if you've worked through this book, you've already done them all—and more. So, go get that badge!

ORGANIZE A FAMILY REUNION

Sometimes you can make the evidence come to you. Family stories, family recipes, family treasures, and ... family. It takes a bit of planning, but you can have your family gather together for a reunion. We're not talking just the family members who always get together for holidays. We're talking about those second and third cousins you've only met a few times in your life. It's time to round them all up, feast on favorite family recipes, and share stories. Here are some tips for planning a family reunion:

1. TEAMWORK

Get a few other family members involved in the planning. Maybe choose some cousins who live in different places. Having more people involved in planning will create more buzz about the event. (It also makes it easier!) Decide who's going to do what: communicating with people, arranging the location, and so on.

2. WHEN AND WHERE

Pick a time and place that is easiest for people, and make it far enough in advance (maybe a whole year!) that people have time to plan. You may not be able to get everyone, but advance notice and convenience will increase your chances.

3. GET THE WORD OUT

Send out a "save the date" notice by email and postcard well in advance. If your parents are cool with it, invite people to join a private social-networking page to receive updates about plans.

4. ASK FOR INPUT

Find out if people would like to make the reunion a potluck picnic, a catered affair, or other type of festive event.

5. WHAT TO DO

Plan activities that people of many ages can join. In addition to a big feast, bring some games along. Softball, volleyball, and Frisbee are good outdoor options. For indoors, think of activities that make people interact. Play a "get acquainted" game, such as taping the name of a famous person on everyone's back and making them guess it by asking other people "yes" and "no" questions. Get a really long piece of paper and draw a timeline on it with dates spanning the last century. Ask people to add milestones in their lives to the timeline.

DID YOU KNOW?

In 2012, a family reunion of the Porteau-Boileve family in Vendée, France, included 4,514 family members! Jean-Michel Cheneau, a direct descendant, traced the family tree back to the 17th century.

6. GATHER EVIDENCE

Ask everyone to bring a favorite family photo, recipe, and/or story to share. You can collect them and promise to share them with everyone afterward.

7. DOCUMENT THE EVENT

Take pictures of everyone who comes, and try to get some group photos. Take several candid (not posed) pictures, too. They often capture the best memories. (Maybe one of your cousins is a good photographer and can be in charge of getting the photos.) Write down everyone's name and address, if you don't already have them.

8. SHARE

With people's permission, share pictures on a *private* social-networking or photo-sharing page. Ask people to share some memories from the reunion on the page.

CASE FILES

BECOMING MORE DIVERSE

DURING THE GLOBAL DEPRESSION OF THE 1930s AND WORLD WAR II (1939–1945), IMMIGRATION TO THE UNITED STATES PLUNGED—BIG TIME. In 1930, foreign-born residents made up 11.6 percent of the U.S. population, but by 1950, they made up only 6.9 percent. In some years, more people left the United States than arrived! After World War II ended, immigration began to rise again. Some U.S. soldiers returned with European wives, and the United States opened up to European refugees and Cubans fleeing the new communist regime in their home country (after 1959).

It wasn't until 1965 that a new wave of immigration to the United States truly began. In that year, Congress passed the Immigration and Nationality Act, ending the preferences for European immigrants. The new law favored relatives of U.S. residents, people with skills the country needed, and refugees fleeing bad situations. The impact of the new law was huge.

Before the 1965 law, most immigrants were European. But during the 1970s, that pattern changed. Now, most immigrants came from Latin America and Asia. Though the 1965 law limited how many could come, 18 million legal immigrants came to the United States over the next three decades, triple the number of the preceding 30 years. In the first decade of the 2000s, more than three-fourths of new arrivals to the United States were from Latin America and Asia.

DID YOU KNOW?

If your family uses a Spanish naming custom, you are so lucky! Children from Spanish-speaking countries often have two family names. The first is usually the father's first surname, and the second is the mother's first surname. While many genealogical detectives search for years—often without success—to find ancestors' maiden names, yours may be as close as your signature.

RESEARCHING RECENT IMMIGRANTS

The year 1965 may seem like a long time ago, but it's really not. It's recent enough that many important genealogical documents—such as federal census records, naturalization records, and more—are too recent to be released. If your family members were in the wave of immigrants who've come to the United States since 1965, you'll need to use different detective skills than genealogists tracing immigrants from long ago. Concentrate on what you can learn from family members. Look through anything you have at home that might tell you about your family's past, and interview relatives here and, if possible, back in the country where your family used to live. If you're looking for documents, the best bets are Social Security documents for ancestors who have died. Locate their Social Security Death Index record and then use that to request a copy of their Social Security application (for a fee). To obtain many other records from the federal government, you may need a parent to file a Privacy Act (PA) request, if the document is about you, or a Freedom of Information Act (FOIA) request, if it is about someone else. Be aware that privacy requirements prevent the government from releasing some documents in certain circumstances. PA and FOIA requests may cost a little money, so this is definitely a time to read the fine print! And, don't forget, you're not alone. Reach out to specialized genealogical groups researching the same country as your ancestor's original home. You may find some great tips.

GET SMART FAST

INVESTIGATE	CLUES
Social Security Death Index Online at FamilySearch.org, Ancestry.com and other sites	For people who died after 1962, possibly Social Security number, name, date of birth and death, residence at time of application, location where death benefits paid
Genealogical societies tied to specific countries or ethnic groups	Search the Internet using the name of country or ethnic group, "historical" or "genealogical," and "society."
Countries and their Cultures: Multicultural America everyculture.com/multi	Articles with overview of countries, information about immigration to the United States, settlement patterns, cultural traditions, and more

FUN FACT

Zhang is the 472nd most common surname in the United States, but it's the fastest climbing. In 2010, it was more than twice as common as it was in 2000, according to the U.S. census.

MEET A FAMILY HISTORIAN & GENEALOGIST

Name: John Philip Colletta
Languages: English, French, Russian, Italian, Latin
Education: Seven degrees and certificates, including a Ph.D. and two master's degrees
Hobbies: Biking, especially around Europe, other outdoor activities, and going to the theater and opera

HE'S KNOWN AS "GENEALOGY JOHN." He's authored three books and dozens of articles on genealogy and family history, teaches at two genealogy institutes, and flies around the country giving speeches and interviews for podcasts, radio, and television. How'd he become such a great genealogical detective? He started when he was a kid—with a notebook, curiosity about his heritage, and mysteries to solve. We interviewed him to learn his tips for successful sleuthing.

HOW DID YOU GET STARTED RESEARCHING YOUR FAMILY HISTORY?

One summer, I was moping around the house. I didn't know what to do with myself. Mom said, "Make a family tree." She drew the chart for me, and she sent me off to my grandparents. So, at the age of 13, I interviewed Mom's mother (her father was deceased already) and Dad's parents. It was a lot of fun.

Mom's maiden name is Ring, and nobody had any idea where that branch of the family came from. So part of the detective work, part of the mystery, was to try to figure out, What about the Rings? Where did they come from?

BACK THEN, PEOPLE WANTED TO PROVE THEIR ANCESTORS WERE AMONG THE EARLIEST SETTLERS IN AMERICA. WHAT ABOUT YOU?

I kind of was hoping my Ring line would go back to the *Mayflower*—or maybe back to colonial Virginia. So when I finally discovered that Mom's great-grandfather Ring was born in France, I was so disappointed. My earliest immigrant ancestors came to America in 1830. The more I got into it, of course, the more I took pride in my own heritage and the more fun I had learning about my own ancestors in Bavaria, Sicily, Alsace-Lorraine, Switzerland ... before there even was a United States of America!

WHAT'S THE BEST PART OF RESEARCHING A FAMILY HISTORY?

The detective work. The great fun is the discoveries. It is unearthing long-lost, forgotten facts about people, places, events. That's what, I think, attracts most people to genealogy. We love the hunt. We love digging into old records, putting the pieces together, and coming up with the lives of people who lived before us. The more you discover about your ancestors, the more you discover about yourself. That's why I call it a journey of self-discovery.

HOW SHOULD SOMEONE WEIGH THE CLUES THEY FIND?

The genealogist is a detective. We need to be skeptical of everything we hear and read. There are mistakes in the old records. And most family stories are not totally accurate, either. So being skeptical is extremely important. But remember: There's a kernel of truth in every family story ... or there would be no story!

WHAT ARE THE BIGGEST OBSTACLES PEOPLE FACE?

Every group has its history and its challenges. Whatever your background is, you're bound to face challenges finding the records and interpreting them. For many Americans, the biggest stumbling block is discovering their ancestors' native towns from overseas and then climbing the family tree in the records created there. They're not written in English, of course. The other big obstacle is cultural. Family sleuths must always ask, "What does this information mean for this culture in this particular time and place?"

YOU EMPHASIZE THE IMPORTANCE OF SETTING GOALS FOR A GENEALOGICAL INVESTIGATION. WHY IS THAT?

A lot of people go online and they click here, they click there, they link from site to site, with no clear goal in mind. You have to establish a goal or your research is scattered and you end up with no satisfying result. Decide, too, what the scope of your quest will be, because you can't do it all. When you reach one goal, then you can move on to the next. There's always more to learn.

WORDS GENEALOGISTS NEED TO KNOW

Alien a foreigner, especially someone who is not a citizen of the country where he or she is living

Archaic something used in an earlier time, but rarely used today

Beneficiary someone who benefits by the provisions of another person's will

Census an official count, such as of a population, that includes related information for government planning

Chronological something arranged in the order of time

Citation formal notation of the source of information

Collateral relative someone with whom you share a common ancestor but who is not in a direct line

Corroboration evidence that confirms or supports another finding

Decedent a person who has died

Deed a legal document used to transfer something, like property

Derivative something based on another source

Descendant the opposite of ancestor; a person descended from a specific ancestor

Draft a system for selecting people for required military service

Emancipation the end of legalized slavery

Enumeration district an area assigned to a census taker for counting

Equinox the time when the sun crosses Earth's Equator, making night and day about the same length all over the planet

Estate everything a person has, especially property, at the time that person dies

Final papers a statement certifying someone meets the requirements for U.S. citizenship, the informal name for a Petition for Naturalization

First papers a sworn statement by someone who intends to become a citizen of a country, the informal name for a Declaration of Intention

Fugitive a person who has escaped a place or is in hiding

Given name usually a person's first and middle names, the ones given you at birth (or baptism), sometimes called "Christian name"

Great Migration a time, starting in the early 1900s, when more than six million African Americans moved from the rural South to cities in the Northeast, Midwest, and West. The term is also used to refer to the migration of Europeans to the American colonies in the 1600s (and other migrations elsewhere).

Inheritance something passed from person to another, often after the person dies

Lineage a line of people descended directly from an ancestor

Maiden name a woman's surname from when she grew up

Manifest a document that lists a ship's passengers and cargo

Manumit to voluntarily release someone from slavery

FIND OUT MORE

WEBSITES

Australian Genealogy and Family History Resources
kindredtrails.com/australia.html

Can Genealogy (sources in Canada)
cangenealogy.com

CanadaGenWeb for Kids Project
rootsweb.ancestry.com/~cangwkid

Cyndi's List: Kids, Teens & The Next Generation
cyndislist.com/kids

Family Tree Kids
kids.familytreemagazine.com/kids/welcome.asp

Irish Ancestors (with links to many resources)
johngrenham.com

Online Genealogy Records and Resources
deathindexes.com/sites.html

United Kingdom (England, Scotland, Wales) and Ireland record links
allenglishrecords.com
genealogy-of-uk.com

BOOKS

Are You Related to a Rock Star? A Guide to Unlocking Your Secret Family History. By Kris Hirschmann (Scholastic, 2011)

A Kid's Guide to Genealogy series. Multiple books by various authors (Mitchell Lane Publishers, 2011)

Your Family Tree series. Multiple books by Jim Ollhoff (ABDO, 2010)

FREE FORMS

Family tree charts – free and interactive
genealogy.about.com/od/free_charts/ig/genealogy_charts/pedigree_chart.htm

Family Tree Magazine – 61 Free Genealogy forms
familytreemagazine.com/FREEFORMS

Markers in genetics, specific parts of DNA that scientists can identify and measure

Maternal on the mother's side

Muster roll a listing of officers and enlisted personnel in a military unit

Paternal on the father's side

Pension a regular payment a person receives after retiring from work

Repository a place—such as an archives, library, courthouse, or museum—where things are stored for safekeeping

Secondary source an account of an event recorded after the event occurred and by someone not directly involved in it

Solstice either of two times during the year when the sun is farthest from the Equator. When it's farthest north, in summer, it produces the longest day (in terms of sunlight) in the Northern Hemisphere; when it's farthest south, in winter, it produces the shortest day.

Transcript a word-for-word exact copy of a text or recording

Ultimate when it's abbreviated (ult.) before a date, it refers to the previous month

Will a legal document that says what someone wants done with his or her possessions after the person's death

Witness someone who sees an event take place. It's also someone who swears that a legal document was signed while he or she watched.

INDEX

PHOTO CREDITS

Cover (tree), Susan Crawford; (DNA), Dabarti CGI/Shutterstock; (paper family), zahar2000/iStockphoto/Getty Images; back cover, Bettmann Archive/Getty Images; 2-3, DNF-StyleiStockphoto/Getty Images; 4, gdvcom/Shutterstock; 5 (UP RT), Maxiphoto/iStockphoto/Getty Images; 5 (UP LE), Mauro Fermariello/Science Photo Library RM/Getty Images; 5 (LO), Blend Images - JGI/Jamie Grill/Brand X/Getty Images; 6, family tree artwork courtesy Erika Horne/www.kithandkinusa.com 10, kevinjeon00/iStockphoto/Getty Images; 11, Library of Congress Prints and Photographs Division; 14-15, Image Source/Photodisc/Getty Images; 16, Andrew Bret Wallis/Digital Vision/Getty Images; 17 (UP), Tim Kitchen/The Image Bank/Getty Images; 17 (LO), Fertnig/iStockphoto/Getty Images; 17, Alan Collins/Alamy Stock Photo; 18 (UP), DNF-Style/iStockphoto/Getty Images; 18 (LO), Lighthunter/Shutterstock; 18 (CTR), Oksun70/Dreamstime; 19 (UP), Gillian Laub/Stone Sub/Getty Images; 19 (LO), Peter Kotoff/Shutterstock; 20 (UP), Richard G. Bingham II/Alamy Stock Photo; 21, magicoven/Shutterstock; 22, aurorat/iStockphoto/Getty Images; 23 (CTR), Tetra Images/Alamy Stock Photo; 23 (LO), Schomburg Center for Research in Black Culture, Manuscripts, Archives and Rare Books Division/The New York Public Library; 24 (UP), Library of Congress Prints and Photographs Division; 24 (LO), Library of Congress Prints and Photographs Division; 25 (UP), Chris Howes/Wild Places Photography/Alamy Stock Photo; 25 (CTR), Library of Congress Prints and Photographs Division; 25 (LO), The U.S. National Archives and Records Administration; 27 (LO), MBI/Alamy Stock Photo; 28 (LO), PhotoAlto sas/Alamy Stock Photo; 29, Hannamariah/Shutterstock; 30, Studio-Annika/iStockphoto/Getty Images; 31, Bart Sadowski/Shutterstock; 31 (LO B), Library of Congress Prints and Photographs Division; 31 (LO A), Charles N. Payne/Library of Congress Prints and Photographs Division; 32 (UP), The New York Public Library; 32 (LO), kansasphoto/Creative Commons; 33 (UP LE), Illustrations from the Nuremberg Chronicle, by Hartmann Schedel (1440-1514); 33 (LO), Canadian Illustrated News, Reproduced from Library and Archives Canada's website: Canadian Illustrated News, 1869-1883.; 33 (UP RT), Inha Makeyeva/Shutterstock; 34, ilbusca/iStockphoto/Getty Images; 34 (white wrinkled paper), Stephen Rees/Shutterstock; 35 (LE), Kenny Tong/Shutterstock; 35 (spiral paper), My Life Graphic/Shutterstock; 36-37, AleksandarNakic/iStockphoto/Getty Images; 38, Tomwang112/iStockphoto/Getty Images; 39 (UP RT), Pictac/iStockphoto/Getty Images; 39 (UP LE), Meinzahn/iStockphoto/Getty Images; 39 (CTR), Photographer/Shutterstock; 39 (LO), Smiltena/Shutterstock; 40, Binh Thanh Bui/Shutterstock; 41 (CTR), stephanie phillips/E+/Getty Images; 41 (LO), shutter_m/iStockphoto/Getty Images; 41 (UP LE), Bara22/Shutterstock; 41 (CTR), Roman Milert/Dreamstime; 42 (UP), Pavel Bobrovskiy/Shutterstock; 44 (CTR LE), Imagno/Gerhard Trumler/Hulton Archive/Getty Images; 44 (CTR RT), igi Cipelli/Archivio Pigi Cipelli/Mondadori Portfolio/Getty Images; 44 (LO), Dorottya Mathe/Shutterstock; 46 (LO), Science Photo Library RM/Getty Images; 47 (LO), sittipong/Shutterstock; 47 (UP), The U.S. National Archives and Records Administration; 48, TonyBaggett/iStockphoto/Getty Images; 49 (UP LE), Granger .com – All rights reserved; 50, North Wind Picture Archives/Alamy Stock Photo; 51 (LO LE), DEA/G. Dagli Orti/DeAgostini/Getty Images; 51 (LO RT), Ira Block /National Geographic Creative; 52-53, Kerrick/iStock-photo/Getty Images; 54, jtphilips/iStockphoto/Getty Images; 55 (LO), Takahiro Igarashi/Image Source/Getty Images; 55 (UP), olgatroy1/iStockphoto/Getty Images; 56 (LO LE), Danny E Hooks/Shutterstock; 56 (UP LE), Monkey Business Images/Dreamstime; 57 (LO), milos-kreckovic/iStockphoto/Getty Images; 57 (UP LE), Chones/Shutterstock; 57 (UP RT), Elena Schweitzer/Shutterstock; 57 (CTR), FotografiaBasica/E+/Getty Images; 57 (UP RT), Elena Schweitzer/Shutterstock; 57 (CTR RT), Wavebreakmediamicro/Dreamstime; 58 (UP), Mark Bowden/iStockphoto/Getty Images; 58 (LO), Grumpy59/iStockphoto/Getty Images; 59 (CTR), Historic Map Works LLC/Getty Images; 59 (LO), Library of Congress Prints and Photographs Division; 59 (UP), Dejan Stanisavljevic/iStockphoto/Getty Images; 60, claudio.arnese/iStock-photo/Getty Images; 61 (CTR), Trinacria Photo/Shutterstock; 61 (UP), Christopher Futcher/iStockphoto/Getty Images; 63, valentinrussanov/E+/Getty Images; 63, YAY Media AS/Alamy Stock Photo; 64, George Wilhelm/Los Angeles Times via/Getty Images; 65 (UP), Susanna Price/Dorling Kindersley/Getty Images; 65 (LO), Linda Steward/iStockphoto/Getty Images; 65 (CTR), MoosyElk/iStockphoto/Getty Images; 66, Imgorthand/E+/Getty Images; 67 (UP RT), davincidig/iStockphoto/Getty Images; 67 (CTR), SolStock/iStockphoto/Getty Images; 67 (LO LE), aldomurillo/iStockphoto/Getty Images; 67 (LO CTR), Photographer/iStockphoto/Getty Images; 67 (UP LE), gdvcom/Shutterstock; 68 (LO), mtlapcevic/iStockphoto/Getty Images; 68 (UP LE), Gertan/Shutterstock; 68 (CTR), somchai rakin/Shutterstock; 68 (UP RT), Willard/iStockPhoto; 68 (UP CTR), Pixelrobot/Dreamstime; 69 (UP), PA Images/Alamy Stock Photo; 69 (LO), LH Images/Alamy Stock Photo; 69 (CTR), Rebecca Hale/NG Staff; 70, Ron Levine/Digital Vision/Getty Images; 71, Rana Faure/Corbis RM Stills/Getty Images; 72, Lewis Wickes Hine/Library of Congress Prints and Photographs Division; 73 (UP), George Grantham Bain Collection/Library of Congress Prints and

Photographs Division; 73 (LO RT), Library of Congress Prints and Photographs Division; 74-75, Mike_kiev/Dreamstime; 76, Carol M. Highsmith Archive/Library of Congress Prints and Photographs Division; 79 (CTR LE), ArTono/Shutterstock; 79 (CTR RT), Studio DMM Photography/Shutterstock; 79 (LO CTR), CK Dessins/Shutterstock; 79 (LO LE), Library of Congress Prints and Photographs Division; 79 (LO RT), Yuriy Boyko/Shutterstock; 79 (UP), vesna cvorovic/Shutterstock; 80 (UP), powerofforever/iStockphoto/Getty Images; 80 (LO), c.byatt-norman/Shutterstock; 81 (UP LE), whitemay/iStockphoto/Getty Images; 81 (LO RT), Stu49/iStockphoto/Getty Images; 81 (CTR), vuralyavas/iStockphoto/Getty Images; 81 (LO), Roberto A Sanchez/Digital Vision Vectors/Getty Images; 82, Lori Epstein/NG Staff; 83 (LO), bloomua/Shutterstock; 84, Radius Images/Alamy Stock Photo; 85 (CTR), Highwaystarz-Photography/iStockphoto/Getty Images; 85 (LO), Timoxa33/iStockphoto/Getty Images; 85 (UP), Lasse Kristensen/Shutterstock; 86, Hill Street Studios/Blend Images/Getty Images; 88 (LO LE), Maxiphoto/iStockphoto/Getty Images; 89 (UP LE), Leonsbox/iStockphoto/Getty Images; 89 (CTR), MWCPhoto/iStockphoto/Getty Images; 89 (LO), Artfoliophoto/iStockphoto/Getty Images; 89 (UP RT), Poznyakov/Dreamstime; 90 (LO), traveler1116/iStockphoto/Getty Images; 90 (UP), Granger.com – All rights reserved; 91 (UP LE), Granger.com; 92-93, Photononstop/SuperStock 94, stocknshares/Getty Images; 95 (CTR), Roy Mehta/Iconica/Getty Images; 95 (LO), lvcandy/DigitalVision Vectors/Getty Images; 95 (UP), artstock/Alamy Stock Photo; 96 (RT), Library of Congress Prints and Photographs Division; 96 (LE), The U.S. National Archives and Records Administration; 98 (LO), North Wind Picture Archives; 98 (CTR RT), North Wind Picture Archives; 98 (CTR LE), North Wind Picture Archives; 99 (UP LE), Photographer/Shutterstock; 99 (LO LE), Its design/Shutterstock; 99 (LO RT), Getty Images Plus/iStockphoto/Getty Images; 99 (UP RT), North Wind Picture Archives; 99 (UP CTR), North Wind Picture Archives; 99 (CTR), North Wind Picture Archives; 99 (UP LE), Photographer/Shutterstock; 99 (LO LE), Its design/Shutterstock; 99 (LO RT), Getty Images Plus/iStockphoto/Getty Images; 100, Gary Blakeley/Shutterstock; 101 (LO), Radius Images/Alamy Stock Photo; 102, The U.S. National Archives and Records Administration; 103 (LO), Jeff Spicer/Getty Images; 103 (CTR), duncan1890/E+/Getty Images; 103 (UP), The U.S. National Archives and Records Administration; 104, Photodisc; 105 (LO LE), Diane Macdonald/iStockphoto/Getty Images; 105 (CTR RT), AR Images/Shutterstock; 105 (CTR LE), Sabina Dimitriu/Shutterstock; 105 (LO RT), Robert Harding/robertharding/Getty Images; 105 (UP), Mark Thiessen/NG Staff; 106 (UP), kostudio/Shutterstock; 106 (LO), State Library and Archives of Florida; 107, The Art Archive/REX/Shutterstock108 (LE), Sylvain Sonnet/Photolibrary RM/Getty Images; 108 (RT), Comstock; 110 (LO), Elke Van de Velde/Photodisc/Getty Images; 110 (UP), Cheryl E. Davis/Shutterstock; 111 (LO), Karl Schatz/Aurora Creative/Getty Images; 112, Carol M. Highsmith Archive/Library of Congress Prints and Photographs Division; 113 (LO), I. Pilon/Shutterstock; 114 (LO RT), Africa Studio/Shutterstock; 114 (LE), filo/DigitalVision Vectors/Getty Images; 115 (LO LE), Elzbieta Sekowska/Shutterstock; 115 (UP), PamelaJoeMcFarlane/E+/Getty Images; 115 (LO RT), fstop123/E+/Getty Images; 116, Manuscripts and Archives Division/The New York Public Library; 117 (LO), AG-PHOTOS/Shutterstock; 117 (UP LE), The Miriam and Ira D. Wallach Division of Art, Prints and Photographs/The New York Public Library; 118-119, lovro77/E+/Getty Images; 120, The Miriam and Ira D. Wallach Division of.Art, Prints and Photographs/The New York Public Library; 121 (LO LE), Bettmann Archive/Getty Images; 121 (LO RT), Library of Congress Prints and Photographs Division; 122 (LE), Manuscripts and Archives Division/The New York Public Library; 122 (RT), The U.S. National Archives and Records Administration; 123 (UP), Laborant/Shutterstock; 124 (UP), AllaR15/Shutterstock; 124 (LO), burakpekakcan/iStockPhoto; 125 (LO), FotografiaBasica/iStockphoto/Getty Images; 125 (UP LE), picturepartners/Shutterstock; 125 (CTR LE), Kushniarevich Yuliya/Shutterstock; 125 (UP RT), kali9/E+/Getty Images; 125 (CTR), Stieglitz/iStockphoto/Getty Images; 126 (LO), MPI/Getty Images; 126 (CTR), The U.S. National Archives and Records Administration; 127 (UP), The U.S. National Archives and Records Administration; 128 (LO LE), NickS/E+/Getty Images; 128 (UP), Library of Congress Prints and Photographs Division; 129 (LO), vitapix/iStockphoto/Getty Images; 130 (LE), The U.S. National Archives and Records Administration; 130 (RT), The U.S. National Archives and Records Administration; 131 (UP), Allkindza/Getty Images; 132 (LO), Rupert Sagar-Musgrave/Alamy Stock Photo; 132 (UP), Lori Epstein/NG Staff; 133 (LO), PM Images/The Image Bank/Getty Images; 133 (UP), Dmitriy Shironosov/Dreamstime; 134 (UP), ValuykinS/iStockphoto/Getty Images; 134 (LO), Lori Epstein/NG Staff; 135 (UP LE), Donald Erickson/iStockphoto/Getty Images; 135 (LO), TPopova/iStockphoto/Getty Images; 135 (CTR), Patti McConville/Alamy Stock Photo; 135 (LO), Lori Epstein/NG Staff; 136, mg7/iStockphoto/Getty Images; 137 (UP LE), Chicago History Museum/Getty Images; 138, MPI/Getty Images; 139 (UP LE), Schomburg Center for Research in Black Culture, Jean Blackwell Hutson Research and Reference Division/The New York Public Library; 140-141, Andrea Danti/Shutterstock; 142, Jose Luis Pelaez Inc/Blend Images/Getty Images; 143 (UP), iStockphoto/Getty Images; 143 (CTR), RuslanGuzov/iStockphoto/Getty Images; 143 (LO), martin-dm/E+/Getty Images; 144, ZUMA Press, Inc/Alamy Stock Photo; 145 (LO), Nir Alon/Alamy Stock Photo; 146, FatCamera/E+/Getty Images; 147 (LO), yasinguneysu/Getty Images; 147 (UP), Newsies Media/Alamy Stock Photo; 147 (LO LE), Boy Scouts of America; 148 (UP), Yellow Dog Productions/Taxi/Getty Images; 148 (LO LE), AndreyCherkasov/iStockphoto/Getty Images; 148 (LO RT), Ekaterina Minaeva/Alamy Stock Photo; 149 (CTR LO), Joe_Potato/iStockphoto/Getty Images; 149 (UP), Liliboas/E+/Getty Images; 149 (CTR UP), andresr/Getty Images; 149 (LO), Image Source/Digital Vision/Getty Images; 150, The Miriam and Ira D. Wallach Division of Art, Prints and Photographs/The New York Public Library; 151 (LO), Mohammed Elshamy/Anadolu Agency/Getty Images; 152 (paper), vesna cvorovic/Shutterstock; (magnifying glass), Vitaly Korovin/Shutterstock; (pencil), Boltenkoff/Shutterstock; (paper clip), Andrew Scherbackov/Shutterstock; (old paper), revers/Shutterstock; (open manila folder), David Smart/Shutterstock; (spiral notebook paper), My Life Graphic/Shutterstock;(white wrinkled paper), Stephen Rees/Shutterstock

ACKNOWLEDGMENTS & CREDITS

For my love, Jim, whose dedication to family always warms my heart
—TJR

Since 1888, the National Geographic Society has funded more than 12,000 research, exploration, and preservation projects around the world. The Society receives funds from National Geographic Partners, LLC, funded in part by your purchase. A portion of the proceeds from this book supports this vital work. To learn more, visit natgeo.com/info.

NATIONAL GEOGRAPHIC and Yellow Border Design are trademarks of the National Geographic Society, used under license.

For more information, visit nationalgeographic.com, call 1-800-647-5463, or write to the following address:

National Geographic Partners
1145 17th Street N.W.
Washington, D.C. 20036-4688 U.S.A.

Visit us online at nationalgeographic.com/books

For librarians and teachers: ngchildrensbooks.org

More for kids from National Geographic: kids.nationalgeographic.com

For information about special discounts for bulk purchases, please contact National Geographic Books Special Sales: specialsales@natgeo.com

For rights or permissions inquiries, please contact National Geographic Books Subsidiary Rights: bookrights@natgeo.com

Designed by Project Design Company

National Geographic supports K–12 educators with ELA Common Core Resources. Visit natgeoed.org/commoncore for more information.

Trade paperback ISBN: 978-1-4263-2983-8
Reinforced library binding ISBN: 978-1-4263- 2984-5

The author wants to thank the creative and dedicated National Geographic Kids Books team for making this book amazing: Priyanka Lamichhane, senior editor; Jen Agresta, project editor (whose unflagging enthusiasm made this doubly fun); Brett Challos, art director; Lori Epstein, photo director; Project Design Company; Joan Gossett, editorial production manager; Anne LeongSon and Gus Tello, design production assistants; and Robin Palmer, fact checker.

Printed in China
17/RRDS/1